T0153003

*Praise for Pattiann Rogers*

"We read her works, sentence by sentence, image by image, and return to all that is beautiful, mysterious, and erotic."
— **Terry Tempest Williams**

"If angels were to agree upon a language to describe creation, a tone of voice and a point of view that would adequately celebrate the divine, these would be the poems they would write. . . . If this is not poetry in service to humanity, I do not know what is." — **Barry Lopez**

"Rogers writes in that richest indigenous vein of American poetry that combines scientific discovery (particularly natural history) with a sublime, raptured egotism, a tradition stemming from Emerson and Whitman."
— *Hudson Review*

"Here is a celebratory voice in American poetry; her descriptions of the physical world are at once rapturous and visionary; while other poets moan, she soars and sings."
— **Christopher Merrill**

"Pattiann Rogers is one of the most original voices of recent decades. Readers who savor her perceptions, her intricate, vastly intelligent sense of connections, are heartened indelibly—she is a crucial poet for a disconnected time."
— **Naomi Shihab Nye**

"[Rogers] knows so much natural history, and knows it with such exuberance." — *Washington Post*

# The Grand Array

# The Grand Array

*Writings on Nature, Science, and Spirit*

## Pattiann Rogers

Trinity University Press
San Antonio

Published by Trinity University Press
San Antonio, Texas 78212

Cover design by Nicole Hayward
Cover photo: © Franz Lanting/Corbis
Book design by BookMatters, Berkeley

*Library of Congress Cataloging-in-Publication Data*
Rogers, Pattiann, 1940–
The grand array : writings on nature, science, and spirit / by Pattiann Rogers.
   p. cm.
SUMMARY: "This collection of essays by poet Pattiann Rogers written over twenty-five years, along with three interviews from the same period, lays out Rogers's vision of the essential unity and interdependence of science, spirituality, the arts, and the experience of the physical world"—PROVIDED BY PUBLISHER.
ISBN 978-1-59534-067-2 (hardcover : alk. paper)
I. Title.
PS3568.0454G73   2010
814'.54—DC22                           2010002424

14  13  12  11  10     5  4  3  2  1

For my husband, in this year
of our fiftieth wedding anniversary,
September 3, 1960–2010


*Haply I think on thee—and then my state,*
*Like to the lark at break of day arising*
*From sullen earth, sings hymns at heaven's gate:*
*For thy sweet love remember'd such wealth brings*
*That then I scorn to change my state with kings.*

WILLIAM SHAKESPEARE

# Contents

# Introduction

The majority of the eighteen essays gathered here, written over a thirty-year period, represent a response to editors who solicited essays for their respective journals on subjects that they felt I might be interested in addressing. And they were correct. I was not only interested, I enjoyed writing essays on the subjects they suggested. Because of these solicitations, I was given an audience I could imagine easily: the editor and the readers of each particular journal.

I envisioned this audience to be of good readers possessing curiosity about all facets of the physical world and who had affection for the life of the earth, an audience asking questions along with me about the meanings of certain words and the places of these words and their concepts in our lives—*divinity, nature and the natural world, life and death, creator, spirituality, contemporary cosmology, humanity.* I imagined that these good readers were experiencing many of the same conflicts and dilemmas that I was experiencing, the same joys and gifts, and that they would be open to considering differing thoughts and suppositions concerning them.

I like the ways I can explore a subject in prose. Recounting stories or events in my own life has come more easily to me in prose than in poetry. For example, in "Cradle" and " 'For Me Mothers and the Mothers of Mothers . . . ,' " memory and autobiographical detail are employed to a great extent to illustrate the themes introduced, whether describing the beach at Normandy and my reactions to my visit there or appreciating my young son's comments on the beauty of a small catfish he'd captured or recounting my experiences with an abandoned lamb in "Surprised by the Sacred."

Occasionally, I discovered a new perception while writing of a past event. The essay "Born, Again and Again" is an example of this sort of discovery. While writing about my baptism at age thirteen in a small river near my home in Missouri, I discovered an unorthodox way of defining divinity through this flowing river world and its surrounding life. Discovery, something I have always sought in my poetry, has come to me by different routes in prose.

"Surprised by the Sacred" and "Rain" were a joy to write. I loved looking for brief snatches of poems, a few lines by other poets to insert in specially chosen places within these essays, using these poems either to comment on the subject or to expand upon it, to illustrate it or take it in a slightly different direction. I liked what happened when I placed a new voice within the prose, a distinctly different rhythm and sound from my own, yet one that could enhance the aura and bring imagery to the sense of the thesis. I even liked the interruptions to my voice that these poems created. Their gestures and attitudes added an interesting complexity to the pace and tone of the essay as a whole.

"Words in the Age of Stars" similarly uses this technique, although to a slightly different purpose. I interspersed poems about the stars and the night sky throughout this essay as examples to help formulate the major theme. This essay was originally written as a lecture and subsequently modified for publication, as was "Twentieth-Century Cosmology and the Soul's Habitation." These are the only two essays in the collection that were originally lectures. "What among Heavens and Suns" was first an informal talk given from notes at an outdoor gathering of friends and colleagues near Colorado Springs. At one point during this talk, the calls of coyotes were heard in the distance, and they became part of the event and part of the essay.

Music is a basic difference between prose and poetry in my work. That difference plays a role during the writing process and in the final result. When I write essays, I'm talking. The flow of the words contains a cadence and rhythm, but these do not dominate or lead the way in the choice of words or their order, as music does in poetry. In essays, I'm talking to an audience that is listening or reading my words in a particular way, an audience that is expecting to absorb the language in a particular way and expecting to be able to restate, at least partially, the content of the communication.

When I write poetry, I'm singing. An audience reading or listening to poetry is like an audience attending a symphony concert. This audience is expecting a different experience and is listening in a different way, not in the way an audience at a lecture or the reading of a prose narrative is listening. Not only the mind but the body, responding to the music, is engaged in a different way. When listening to music, whether of a symphony orchestra or the reading of a wonderful poem, no audience should expect to be able to intellectualize or articulate to any exact degree what the experience and its content have been. The audience can expect to dwell within those moments of music and its imagery and to retain the sense of the body's response.

Occasionally the distinction between prose cadence and the music of poetry becomes blurred. The essay "'I Hear and Behold God in Every Object, Yet Understand God Not in the Least'" is probably the best example in this collection of this kind of blurring. The prose, in certain sections in this piece, comes very close to the music of poetry. This is a meditative piece, I believe, and the sound and motion of it was created in the first paragraph. That sound and motion enters and departs several times throughout. But this essay is a prose piece, not a poem. It does not draw primarily on the arts and crafts of poetry. It intends to speak in prose, to serve and to take advantage of that form.

The three interviews at the end of this book were conducted over a span of twenty years—the McCann interview (1985), the Doyle interview (2000), and the Johnston interview (2005). An interview is a literary form of its own, distinct from an essay or a poem. These three interviews present together a history and overview of the years when these essays and my poems were being written. They reflect not only some of my views during those years but also the currents of the times and the individual interests and approaches of the interviewers. Each establishes a distinct tone and perspective.

*The Grand Array* addresses in prose the sources that have been at the heart of many of my poems, yet it contains expositions and narratives different from my poetry in manner and in approach to its subjects. Like a stone missing from a mosaic, the vision composed by the separate books of my published work taken together would be incomplete if this book were missing. It is a fact of the landscape, a piece of the portrait, a central element of the scene.

( PART I )

# A Terrible Need

Last night I dreamed I was lying outdoors in an open clear-ing beside a forest. The land, the earth beneath me, was rocking slowly back and forth. I watched the moon directly above me sway behind a few leafless trees and then out into the open sky, a mottled ivory-gray sky with thin and scat-tered clouds, then back again behind the trees. I said to myself in my dream, "I bet nobody has ever seen the moon move like that before." The earth was a cradle, and I was being rocked slowly and steadily, aware, serene and happy.

I don't know where dreams come from, maybe from many places. But I do know I'd been thinking recently about how the earth moves through space. It seems now that not only is the earth rotating on its axis and revolving around our star the sun and moving with the solar system around the center of the Milky Way Galaxy, but it is also moving up and down, like a horse on a carousel, very, very slowly over millions of years. I'd been trying to envision all of these motions and my participation in them, picturing the images we have of Earth from space, trying to grasp the very strangeness of it all. This vision was oddly comforting. The word "gliding" kept occurring to me.

Why comforting? In dark times when human affairs seem impossibly tangled and no certain course of action is evident, in dangerous times filled with hatred, deceit, and ill-will and increased fears for ourselves and our families, it is often comforting to me to move into the realm of the stars, out into that old, old awe-inspiring realm of great expanse and mystery from which the material of our being has come, to picture our earth within the roiling energy of the universe and its innumerable events of light.

In 1990, a photograph of the earth was taken by the *Voyager I* spacecraft as it traveled beyond the orbit of Neptune, the eighth planet from the sun. In this photograph the earth appears as a tiny white pearl barely visible from that distance, a pearl the size of the last pearl on a string of pearls, a tiny orb suspended among a host of stars. Carl Sagan called it a pale blue dot. Everything we value and all of human history is contained on that speck. Glaciers, orchids, apricots, ferns and limestone bluffs, Caesar, Michelangelo, Einstein, the shudder of stampeding herds of horses or wildebeests, the thunder and dust of rolling tanks, dinosaur bones and fossilized forests, grandmothers, grandfathers, the oleander bush in the backyard, the dog asleep beneath it, wild oceans and polar icebergs, everything we touch, everything we hear and taste, all that we trust, all that we cherish, is present on that tiny dot, almost invisible, almost lost, a grain floating in a sea deeper, wider, and darker than we can conceive.

From this perspective, human cruelty to one another, bombs and guns, nuclear weapons, the passion for vengeance or power, seem pathetically childish, absurd, insane.

We are alone on a tiny spot of life in the midst of the vast unknown, the black blindness of space and time, and yet we have been engaged almost continuously in killing one another since the beginning of recorded history. Someone watching us at bloody war with each other on that tiny speck in the universe, the earth cratered by our weapons, would surely shake his head in astonishment. By all reason and known facts, we should be clinging to one another, helping, consoling one another, celebrating together the life and the moment we are given.

Humans are moved by the vision of our earth floating in the immensity of the heavens, surrounded by stars. Whether we are full of wonder or fear, whether we feel diminished or liberated, elated, blessed, or humbled, we see ourselves and our earth anew when we give ourselves to that vision.

Van Gogh in a letter to his brother wrote, "I have . . . a terrible need . . . dare I say the word? . . . of religion. Then I go out at night and paint the stars." We have his remarkable painting *The Starry Night* as a result. Contemplation of the stars has been a steady presence in most human cultures of the past and has given rise to religious thoughts, to questions about human existence and our first origins, to reaffirmation of a presence beyond ourselves and yet within ourselves.

Unfortunately, those of us living in this country today rarely see the night sky undimmed by city lights. Thus we are without an extremely important source of inspiration and spiritual reflection that was continually available to our ancestors. Recently a woman living in LA with her family told me that she asked her young daughter how many stars she thought there were. Her daughter answered, "Three." For most of us, it takes some planning and probably a little traveling to reach a place where the night sky can spread above us clear and unobscured from horizon to horizon. I was shocked the last time I had an occasion to witness such a sky. It was over rural Wyoming. I'd forgotten how black the night can be, a black that never stops, and yet how totally filled with stars. Lying on the ground and looking up, I thought I was immersed in the starry body of a creator. I was part of the body of a creative power and being beyond myself. I knew I was being touched everywhere by ancient light that had traveled immense distances to reach me, to enter my eyes and become recognized. I wrote of this in "Why Lost Divinity Remains Lost": ". . . the stars, seeded by an uneven hand, / so profuse, so demanding, so clearly / insistent in their silence."

But we are also fortunate in our time, because we have stories told by our astronomers that increase our amazement of the heavens, stories our ancestors never had an opportunity to hear. Last November my husband and I rose in the middle of the night to witness the Leonid meteor shower. I thought we might be the only ones to leave warm beds on a cold night to watch a few "falling stars." When we arrived at a nearby park, however, I was surprised to see cars lining the roads, and many people, some with coats thrown over their pajamas, standing, watching the skies. All of us, especially the raucous children, thoroughly enjoyed this spectacle, unlike people of the nineteenth century who woke to similar meteor showers in panic and fear, believing the stars were falling and the end of the world was at hand. We knew those bright showers of "falling stars" were the result of the earth passing through the trail of dust particles left behind by the comet Tempel-Tuttle, the dust particles burning as they entered the earth's atmosphere. The sight was exhilarating, because I knew, I could feel, I was riding on the earth, our beautiful racing, spinning earth speeding among all the other moving elements of the universe. I felt again the magic of that vision of our earth traveling through a realm magnificent in its scope.

The vision of the starry heavens has the power to remind us again of who we are, of where we are. By imagining our place in the universe of space and time and holding tight to that image, we might redefine the ultimate nature of the human state, invigorate that definition, proclaim our nature, and dedicate our unique talents once again to praise and to life.

(2003)

# Thoreau and Mothers

I want to write a few words about the female in nature, the female of other species as well as the female of the human species.

When we observe wildlife in a natural setting—coyotes, bear, elk, moose, rabbits, turtles, fish, birds—we can assume that at least half or more of the animals we observe are female, a fact that should be kept in mind. And of these females, practically all are engaged in one stage or another in the bearing and raising of young. Imagine that, that mighty endeavor, an all-consuming festival of procreation—gestation, birth, lactation, protection, nurturing—constantly in progress.

In some species males are involved in caring for the young after birth (birds, seahorses, some canines), but in most mammals males are indifferent to the process and have no relationship with the female after mating nor with their offspring.

So, often the entire tasks of bearing, feeding, and protecting the young fall to the female, a tremendous responsibility, and we all know with what devotion, what indomitable ferocity and courage and physical strength and commitment the female carries out these tasks. We know the dangers, for instance, of getting between a female moose and her calf.

I was particularly struck by this quality of devotion when watching some pet mice we once had. The female mouse, after giving birth, was totally engaged in caring for her offspring. She had a purpose, an important, crucial job, and her actions seemed to carry the sense of this. She was completely energized in feeding her helpless wards, moving them about, stimulating them, hurrying off to a corner of her cage to make new, clean nests, fluffing up cedar chips, arranging them suitably, then moving all the infants to their new abode, cleaning them, checking them, feeding them. With what skill and mastery she carried out these tasks, and her babies grew into perfect seeing, hearing, functioning mice.

Watching that mother mouse, I was tremendously proud to be a female. If you'll forgive a little hyperbole—it seemed to me there was no more important work in the universe than what she was doing.

I want to say a little about Thoreau and what I perceive to be an omission in his work in this regard. I admire Thoreau and love much of his writing. He's a great spirit, and I'm entirely grateful that he lived as he did and wrote of his life as he did.

But I want to point out that the major portion of his work is addressed to a male audience. This is no great discovery on my part. The most superficial reader can detect almost immediately that Thoreau is writing to and for men. I don't blame Thoreau for this. He most probably was correct in assuming that his reading audience would be composed mainly of men, and Thoreau, after all, was in many ways a product of his time and culture, much as he wished to be a total maverick. He wasn't raised in the woods by wolves. He was New England bred, with a Harvard education and friends among the literary elite.

Now the lifestyle that Thoreau recommends in works such as *Walden* and "Walking" would be hard for a man with a family to support to adhere to, but that lifestyle would be absolutely impossible for a woman with dependent children to follow. Impossible. In fact, Thoreau states straightforwardly in "Walking": "If you are ready to leave father and mother and brother and sister, and *wife* and child and friends, and never see them again—if you have paid your debts and made your will and settled all your affairs and are a free *man*, then you are ready for a walk." (The italics are mine.)

Of course, Thoreau had only himself to be concerned about, and he had the support of a large family behind him had he needed to turn to it. But a mother with young children has concerns other than her own. Infants and young children not only require constant supervision, but they must also be fed and clothed and housed and loved, just as Thoreau himself was. This means for some time nursing a child, every four hours, breast or bottle, then actually putting food in the child's mouth, bite by bite, holding the cup to the lips. Raising children means putting arms into sleeves, legs into pants, socks on feet, shoes on feet, buttoning coats and sweaters, tying hats on heads, every day, day in and day out. It means guarding against illness and injury constantly. It means caring for the body of another human being, actually keeping a young and vulnerable body alive. Alive. This is not an insignificant task. It is crucial to the culture, and I haven't even mentioned here the spiritual nurturing of children.

Where is an address to these responsibilities in Thoreau's work? . . . Thoreau, the man who studied nature and must have seen the work involved in seeing to the survival of the young? As far as I can see, these tasks and obligations are not acknowledged or even taken into account in his advocacy of a human lifestyle. Yet in Thoreau's time we might assume that almost all women were involved in one way or another in caring for and raising children. How very strange that these obligations are not acknowledged or dealt with and even stranger that no one mentions now that they are not acknowledged. Some might contend that Thoreau's focus was in another direction, that women and mothers and their lives were not his concern. Fine. Then that needs to be said, and women and mothers who read him should keep that fact in mind.

It might also be said that there is a certain amount of exaggeration in Thoreau's positions, that he simply wishes to make a point about life after the Industrial Revolution and that few take his recommendations literally. Although I'm not sure Thoreau would appreciate such contentions, I can accept them and simply take from Thoreau's work his affirmation of life, his keen observations of the natural world, his grand language, the force of his energy.

But none of this changes the fact that mothers and their responsibilities, responsibilities that cannot be abandoned like a farmer might abandon his fields, are missing from Thoreau's work. This renders the work incomplete, in my opinion, as a recipe for living.

Even today, surrounded in nature as we are by females caring for their young, and with half the human population being women, and perhaps three-fourths of these women, or more, being mothers, still this role is peripheral or absent altogether from consideration in our discussions about the moral life. I'm no longer willing to be silent when I see this role overlooked or dealt with casually or off-handedly in our literature, a literature in which almost all portrayals of mothers have been written by men or by women who were not mothers themselves. Some of the most intense and enduring emotions ever experienced by human beings are the ones felt by mothers toward their children, yet we have few fine and complete artistic accounts of these emotions written by mothers themselves.

I'm no longer willing to overlook the role of mothers in any discussion of our moral and ethical responsibilities, because to overlook it means not to take seriously, intellectually seriously, the raising of children. That's a tragedy, in my opinion, for our children, our literary tradition, and for the health of our society.

(1992)

# Fury and Grace

Shoal Creek, near Joplin, Missouri, where I grew up, is, for me, the archetype of all creeks. We went to see Shoal Creek often when I was young, like visiting a highly interesting acquaintance who lived a strange but purposeful life. The creek was always there, more or less in its same place, doing its mud-and-fish, worn-rock-and-ruffled-rapids, racing act.

I could wade through the clear waters where it widened near a small dam, bend down, and look from my world through a silver, reflective boundary into a world that was forced to remain within that boundary—tiny black snails like spots on the stones, fat tadpoles that seemed just heads with wispy tails, crawdads propelling backward to hide beneath muddy leaves and muck, olive-green minnows so narrow and rock-colored that they were almost invisible until they flicked and moved as one body from sun to shadow.

And when I looked up again into the world of air and sky, it seemed I had been existing in another life, among alien creatures whom I nevertheless knew and regarded with respect.

I occasionally swam in Shoal Creek, learning of it in

another way, standing waist-deep in its murky water, push-ing against its force on my body, or sitting in its shallow rapids making it rear up, ruffle and surge against my back. Who was it? It came and went constantly yet was always present.

McClellan Park was situated on a steep hill, a high cliff above Shoal Creek, a cliff covered with rocky bluffs and caves typical of the area. A picnic at McClellan Park always involved a precarious hike down the hill, everyone slipping on rocks and gravel, skidding and grabbing bushes and trees to keep from falling. I held onto my dad. At the bot-tom we would walk for a while beside the creek, which ran close to the hill, pressing against the rise of land. My dad skipped rocks over the surface of the water, big leaps and then smaller. My brother and I tried.

A favorite story of my dad's was the time my brother, six years old, started running down the hill and couldn't stop, shouting and yelling. My dad, running after him barely grabbed him by one arm, swinging him out over the creek just before he would have plunged into its deep, rushing waters.

Once we went in the rain to see Shoal Creek mad and powerful, high over its banks, its white froth climbing and fighting against the thick poplars marking its old boundar-ies. It rolled and thrashed over its single-lane bridge. We were consigned to viewing the flooding from one side, many cars lined up before the impassable crossing. People in rain-coats and boots stood around outside their cars watching in amazement, proclaiming in low voices, with reverence and respect, as if Shoal Creek were justified in this show of frightening rebellion.

But I love Shoal Creek most, I think, because I first learned about the bodies of boys while parked beside it at the end of dirt fishing lanes, the sound of its life continually cresting and flowing, swelling and rhythmic in the background among the whispers and laughters and joys of those nights. The affirmation and promise of moving water has been present with me since, in everything I've ever experienced of sexual love.

The being and cadence of Shoal Creek is part of who I am, defining both fury and grace, influencing the pace of my passions, shaping the undercurrent of my sleep, resonant always in the waking motion and music of my language and my thought.

(1999)

# Places within Place

A poplar stands outside the east window of our upstairs bedroom in the place where I now live, where I have lived for the past eight years. This tree has been part of my waking and part of my sleeping for most of the nights and days of these years. The sound of its leaves turning in the batter of hard rain or wind, or dripping with the fall of lighter moisture, or its branches silent with the rigid silence of zero degrees, have become cadences in my thought and in my thought of possibilities, undercurrents of motion and presence like pulse or breath or passion.

I feel certain that the structure of this poplar against the sky, against the pale of predawn, or catching the sun of dusk, is a factor partially determining the form and pacing of my words, the way I shape the music of my voice, my pleasure in the particular rise and fall of logic or narrative, my interpretation of gesture, my vision of the bones of my stance.

But this tree is not always the same tree. It is not only the poplar of leafless winter, the poplar in snow, encased in ice, the poplar of seeds, full of yellow leaf or with one yellow leaf left, the poplar wounded, leaking dark sap, but it is also the blind poplar I cannot see in fog, the gray and black poplar of night, the white poplar of the moon, the mysterious, rock-shifting subterranean poplar chasing water above the melting core of the earth.

I know it was absolutely not the same tree standing inside the grief of my mother's death as the tree it was outside our window last night during love, as it was a fire rocking with my anger one evening, as it has stood in the way of my hatred, as it has been sharply beautiful with my despair.

And it is also, in truth and actuality, the poplar I imagine it to be, the one possessing a fluttering ghost in each leaf, the messianic poplar suffused with delivered promise, the poplar of a thousand tongues all licking at once inside my ear, the poplar shattered, splintered, and scorched by lightning on the plains before I was born, the poplar I downed with my own ax, the one that fell across my spine and left me face down on the earth.

What is the poplar in the eyes of the June magpie shrieking from its blue branches? What does the poplar become beneath Ursa Major, seven stars on each leaf? Where is the place of the poplar of five years ago, half again as massive? Where precisely *is* the poplar of memory?

What will become of this tree without my designation "poplar," without my announcement of its multiple realities? Devoid of my attentions, is the poplar yet again a different tree? Is it possible to imagine the poplar absent the imagination? If so, then that place might be a new level of the void.

How should we comprehend the place of this particular poplar latched here to this land at this spot and then spun by the earth, carried also by the sun's system, swung round again on the outer rim of the Milky Way galaxy, itself speeding outward? From what place has the poplar come? To what place is it going? Is it necessary to imagine these truths too in order to fully comprehend and appreciate the poplar's present place?

And how does intention interpret this poplar? How does divinity know this tree? What is "benevolence" juxtaposed to a leaf of poplar midsummer?

In one poplar in one moment are a million poplars in a million moments and a million places, places within a place, each singular, each forbearing, each emphatic, all simultaneous in their contradictory and mutually exclusive natures.

How should we define "place"? The word "definition" implies language; the word "place" implies internal and spatial linkages; these then imply one who forges both found and invented connections, which then suggests one who may similarly break, dismiss, reorder, rebuild those connections.

Dare we presume at all to define "poplar"? Dare we presume to define "place"? We do, continually knowing that we ourselves must always be recognized and included as affected observers within our definitions, as the biased creators of definition, simultaneously shaping and being shaped.

We define, even knowing our definitions will be never ending, never secured, always changing, constantly resisting themselves, constantly determining themselves. This is our burden, and this is our blessing.

(1997)

# Words in the Age of Stars

We are all familiar with many images of the earth—its variety of life forms, from one-celled creatures to whales, from the tiniest microbes to soaring sequoias, the many life forms of today, as well as the many extinct life forms of past ages. We have images of the earth's geology, its oceans and mountains, prairies and deserts, ice fields, tundras, images of thunderstorms, snow-filled forests, sunlight and shadows. Most of us know these images intimately by having come into contact with many of them. We are impressed by them and curious about them. This essay is about another phenomenon that surrounds us continuously, one that is not on the earth but is profoundly of the earth—and that is the starry sky.

Nothing else in the physical world evokes exactly the same kind of wonder as the field of stars that we can see clearly on a moonless night, far from city lights. Anyone who truly looks at the panorama of the night heavens almost always feels a sense of awe and wonder and perhaps something of astonishment these days, since so many of us rarely see the night sky unobscured, either by trees or mountains or buildings. We rarely see the entire night sky undimmed by human-made light. When we do have the opportunity to view the night sky unobscured, most of us begin to ask questions. We begin to wonder.

Individuals and cultures of various times have differed in the ways they have wondered about the stars, in the forms and methods their wonderings have taken, and in the expressions of their wonder. They have differed in the questions they asked regarding the stars and in the responses they proposed to those questions. All cultures have been attentive to the stars in their own ways, believing they contain profound meanings for human activities and human thought, that they hold clues to our origins, and that the questions the stars provoke are crucial to our understanding of ourselves.

What feelings do the stars evoke in us, people living in the twenty-first century with a little information about the universe not available to other generations? indifference? curiosity? fear? awe? freedom? gratitude? devotion? a combination of all of these and more? All these contradictory emotions evoked by the presence of the stars and the contemplation of the place of the earth and human beings in this universe have been commonly experienced by many writers and artists. For instance, in a discussion of the work of Stephen Spielberg and Stanley Kubrick, critic Stephen Hunter of the *Washington Post* wrote that Spielberg's worldview is that "Even if it contains killer sharks, the universe ultimately makes sense; it can be known and understood." In the same review, Hunter wrote that Stanley Kubrick's stance, however, is that "The universe is a whirligig of gases and cosmic debris that always conspires to render human nobility and aspiration futile." These two world-views, both occasioned by contemplation of the universe, are contradictory.

Here are examples of several poems and brief prose pieces expressing very different emotions occasioned by the stars, different worldviews. Each piece is by a different writer and is spoken in a different voice by a different sort of person, each with a different background and attitudes, writing in different times and places.

First, in Mark Twain's *Adventures of Huckleberry Finn*, Huck and Jim, on their raft floating down the Mississippi, puzzle one night over the origin of the stars. Huck as narrator relates the following:

> It's lovely to live on a raft. We had the sky, up there, all speckled with stars, and we used to lay on our backs and look up at them, and discuss about whether they was made, or only just happened—Jim he allowed they was made, but I allowed they happened; I judged it would have took too long to make so many. Jim said the moon could a laid them; well that looked kind of reasonable, so I didn't say nothing against it, because I've seen a frog lay most as many, so of course it could be done. We used to watch the stars that fell, too, and see them streak down. Jim allowed they'd got spoiled and was hove out of the nest.

In an entirely different tone and stance, the poem "Evening," by the German poet Rainer Maria Rilke, expresses the conflict of contradictory emotions that a starry night sky can evoke.

*Evening*

The sky puts on the darkening blue coat
Held for it by a row of ancient trees;
you watch; and the lands grow distant in your sight,
one journeying to heaven, one that falls;

and leave you, not at home in either one,
not quite so still and dark as the darkened houses,
not calling to eternity with the passion
of what becomes a star each night, and rises;

and leave you (inexpressibly to unravel),
your life, with its immensity and fear,
so that, now bounded, now immeasurable,
it is alternately stone in you and star.

(from *The Selected Poetry of Rainer Maria Rilke*,
translated by Stephen Mitchell)

Watching the transformation of day into night and the stars becoming gradually visible causes Rilke to contemplate who and what humans are. We humans, he seems to be saying in this poem, are not entirely earth, yet not quite heaven either, now "bounded," yet now "immeasurable." We are left to "unravel" this life, this paradox.

"Star Boys," by Richard Katrovas from his book *Green Dragons*, is yet another expression of the stars, a poem in the voice of a street man, a working man, maybe an unemployed working man. The tone is conversational, in a New Orleans vernacular. The speaker seems to be in a bar talking with a group of friends at night, speaking the wisdom of a bar-room philosopher.

*Star Boys*

All the tough dudes
are whistling in the dark.
Wildman Bob's in Chino.
Dirty Dave's doing time
in his daddy's garage.
Wolf's a woman.
Lizard's got nobody.
Now we all know nothing
really happens, boys.
Things just get perpetrated.
Besides, the sun's a pain
when you're tripping
on what's gone down
and I'd rather stick
my finger in the cool moon.
I'd rather sit and watch
purple curls of smoke
flatten on the ceiling
in the blacklite
chew on salted scallions
pop a couple beers
and think a white wall
till fog comes in early morning
and I can go outside
walk down to the pier
and listen to the birds

and water. But I can't
wait. The stars
are whistling lips
of the dead arranged
in a great tattoo and if
we could back up, boys,
I mean, right out of the universe,
we'd see it's just an anchor,
a naked body, a pierced heart.


A haiku by the early-eighteenth-century Japanese poet
Issa presents another point of view.

A lovely thing to see:
through the paper window's hole,
the Galaxy.

(from *An Introduction to Haiku*,
translated by Harold G. Henderson)


I love the perspective in this poem, the paper window's
hole juxtaposed to the galaxy. What is one to the other?
What significance of each is revealed by this juxtaposition? I wonder what the word "galaxy" meant to Issa in the
eighteenth century, something a little different from what
it means to us now?

Robinson Jeffers expands on the shift in the contemporary definition of the stars and their place in our lives
in "The Epic Stars," from *The Beginning and the End and Other
Poems*.

The heroic stars spending themselves,
Coining their very flesh into bullets for the lost battle,

They must burn out at length like used candles;
And Mother Night will weep in her triumph, taking home
    her heroes.
There is the stuff for an epic poem—
This magnificent raid at the heart of darkness, this lost
    battle—
We don't know enough, we'll never know.
Oh happy Homer, taking the stars and the Gods for granted.


"We don't know enough, we'll never know." And now we can never go back to the stance of Homer, "taking the stars and the Gods for granted," because we understand, we have evidence, that the stars are passing away, the stars are dying. And what of God?

Reflecting yet another approach to the stars, while drawing on a perspective and vocabulary of contemporary astronomy, is the fourth part of a four-part poem of my own titled "Good Heavens."


Good—because the heavy burnings
and fumings of evolving
star clusters and extragalactic
cacophonies—because the flaming
Cygnus Loop, still whipping
and spewing sixty thousand years
after its explosion—because
the churning, disgorging womb
of the Great Nebula and the rushing
oblivions left from the collapse
of protostars—because suffocating
caverns of pulling, sucking gases
and pursuing, encircling ropes

of nuclear bombardments—
because erupting caldrons
of double stars and multiple
stars flinging outward great
spires and towers of searing
poisons—because all of these
for this long have stayed
far, far away from our place.

The vision of the stars and the heavens have enabled many people to achieve new and unique perspectives on the human condition and human events. Many artists, philosophers, and scientists have created new definitions of our place in the universe and from those definitions new interpretations of who we are and to what or to whom we owe our devotions. The universe of stars certainly suggests something greater and grander than ourselves.

Vincent van Gogh stayed up three nights in a row to paint *The Starry Night*. This painting is stunning in its depiction of the energy and color in what others may have deemed a still and serene night sky. The paint on the canvas suggests the exploding stars and swirling galaxies we know now are present throughout the universe.

In letters to his sister, Wilhelmina, written at the same time as he was painting *The Starry Night*, Van Gogh highly recommends the work of Walt Whitman: "I strongly advise you read them (Whitman's poems) because to begin with they are really fine. . . . He sees in the future, and even in the present, a world of healthy, carnal love, strong and frank— of friendship—of work—under the great starlit vault of

heaven a something which after all one can only call God—
and eternity in its place above the world."

Perhaps Van Gogh had read this poem of Whitman's,
"A Clear Midnight," in *From Noon to Starry Night*, a section in
*Leaves of Grass*.

This is thy hour O Soul, thy free flight into the wordless,
Away from books, away from art, the day erased, the lesson
   done.
Thee fully forth emerging, silent, gazing, pondering the
   themes thou lovest best,
Night, sleep, death, and the stars.

For many observers, viewing the night sky inevitably
brings thoughts of divinity, of creation, of mortality, of
beginnings and endings. The following lines from "Star-
Gazing," a poem by Claudius Ptolemaeus, a Greek-Egyptian
living in the second century C.E., are evidence of this human
tendency:

. . . when I gaze upon
The thousandfold circling gyre of the stars,
No longer do I walk on earth
                    but rise
The peer of God himself. . . .

(from *Poems from the Greek Anthology*,
translated by Dudley Fitts)

"Is not God in the height of heaven? and behold the
height of the stars, how high they are!" So Job exclaims the
grandeur and wonder of the stars (22:12).

Moments of realization concerning our place in the universe can come upon us unexpectedly. Isak Dinesen describes the hero of her tale "The Monkey," in *Seven Gothic Tales*, experiencing such a moment as he walks down a corridor of windows in a chateau one night.

> He looked out of one of the windows as he passed it. The moon stood high in the heavens, clear and cold, but the trees of the park and the lawns lay in a silvery mist. There outside was the whole noble blue universe, full of things, in which the earth swam onward amongst thousands of stars, some near and others far away. O world, he thought, O rich world.

The place of the earth within the starry heavens and our visions in our time have been changed by the information and images that have been gathered by astronomers the world over. Recent technological advances allow us to see farther and more clearly into space. How strange are those images of the earth seen from the moon. How can the earth be composed of all the physical lives and beings we experience everyday, those multitudes of life and beings, and at that same time be a small, shining orb surrounded by black, empty silence, the entire earth upon which nothing, no single life, is clearly distinguishable from those distances. How strange that

> . . . the earth can be taut
> with Indian pipe, heavy with matted roots
> of salt marshes, dark with redwood forests,
> deep with shadowed canyons and ocean floors,

while at the very same moment it can soar, clean
and shining, a white and blue grain sailing
in the black heavens around the sun.

(from my poem "The Love of Enchantment:
Felicia Was Kissed in the Garden Last Night")

What does it mean that we of our time have seen the
earth from thousands of miles above it, actual photographs
of the earth taken from thousands of miles away? These
are images of the earth never witnessed by the generations
of people living before us. Do these images imply anything
about the definition of what it means to be human? If so,
what do they imply?

Even more stunning, actually shocking, than those photographs of the earth taken from the moon, is the photograph of the earth taken by *Voyager I* as it passed the orbit
of Neptune on its journey out of the solar system. *Voyager I*
was completing its mission of taking photographs of all the
planets it passed and sending the images back to NASA.
It was destined now to leave the solar system. At this time,
Carl Sagan, present at NASA headquarters, was urging the
scientists to turn Voyager's camera around and take a photograph of the earth from that distance. There was some
reluctance, because turning the camera meant it would then
be facing the sun and there might be damage to its lens.
But the decision was made to take the risk. The camera was
turned and the photograph taken. And there it was, our
Earth, the tiniest dot, smaller than the end of a baby's small
finger, barely visible, even from within our solar system. It

takes imagination and some courage to fully absorb the import of that image.

> Once a photograph of the Earth, taken from the outside, is available . . . a new idea as powerful as any in history will be let loose.
>
> —Sir Fred Hoyle

Chaucer, writing in the twelfth century, presents at the end of *Troilus and Cressida* a view remarkably similar to a contemporary view of the earth and human events. Troilus has been killed by Achilles at the conclusion of the tale, and his spirit begins its ascent into heaven. From that high sphere, Troilus, as spirit, looks back on the earth. Chaucer describes the event in this way:

> Contemptuously the fierce Achilles slew him.
> And when he had been killed his happy spirit
> Rose to the hollow of the seventh sphere,
> Leaving below all earthly elements.
> There in full view he saw the erratic stars
> And heard the sounds of heavenly harmony.
> And down from that high station he began
> To look upon this little spot of earth
> Enfolded by the sea, and with full contempt
> For this unhappy world; he held it all
> A vanity compared with the clear joy
> That is in heaven above; and at the last
> He looked down on the place where he was slain,
> And laughed within himself. . . .

From that vantage point far above Earth, all previous cares and concerns, the sufferings and the joys of human life, and even death, seem petty, insignificant, and laughable to Troilus—and, we must assume, to Chaucer also—Chaucer having placed himself by his imagination in that position high above the earth, witnessing the human condition from a new perspective.

How we envision where we are standing in both time and space has an enormous effect on how we define ourselves as human creatures and consequently a great effect on how we determine our actions and our obligations and how we express our joys and griefs and our hopes. Whether absorbing the vast amount of new information about the universe that has been gathered over the past century or deliberately ignoring it, our present story of the universe, our contemporary cosmology, has pervaded our lives in many ways, and whether we outwardly acknowledge it or not, it has altered our view of the earth and ourselves.

To see the entire earth floating in space is to recognize the earth as one with the universe, immersed in the universe, inseparable from the universe and all of its stellar bodies. There is no barrier between us and all the light and darkness of the universe, all of its history and all of its future. The earth and human beings are participants in the energy of the universe, filled with the same energy as the universe. We believe that the earth and all its life forms, including humans, are made of the dust of old stars, the elements of our bodies having been forged in the nuclear furnaces of past stars. The reasoning and facts behind this assertion have been explained to us. Being physically composed of the same material as the stars binds us forever with the universe.

I can't list here all the ways that human cultures of the past have been affected by the stars, the ways in which they have pondered the night heavens, all the art and literature and religious faiths that have risen from that contemplation, or all the ways that our contemporary world has investigated, explored, and revered the stars and the universe. The birth and evolution of stars, the big bang, countless galaxies, black holes, cosmic dust clouds, asteroid belts, supernovas, pulsars, quasars, comets, star clusters, dark matter—the vision of these elements composing the universe has significance to all human beings.

Like ocean waves striking land or rushing winds in a forest of pine trees or rain rolling over prairie grasses or sharp shadows in a red rock canyon, the stars—seen outdoors away from manmade light, in the sole darkness of a moonless night—have great power to affect the spirit, to expand our vision and our perceptions of ourselves. They evoke emotions not evoked by any other natural phenomena. They cause us to wonder. They seem not to provide answers to some of the most important questions we have, or if they do, we are without the ability to recognize those answers. But they quite obviously imply something about our place and our perceptions, something about creation, something about divinity, about purpose and possibility.

(2003)

# The Great Plains

The dwelling places of my life have always been on or very near the Great Plains of North America. I was raised in the southwest corner of Missouri, only a few miles from the borders of Kansas, Oklahoma, and Arkansas. I moved to Texas when I was twenty-nine and lived there for twenty years. I have resided now for the past ten years in Colorado, just east of the Rockies, on the edge of the Great Plains. While my poems have not always dealt directly with the landscape of the plains, I sense an important influence on my writing of that broad, flat, open, seemingly endless expanse of earth against sky with which I am so familiar.

I agree with the following thoughts from *The American Heritage Book of Indians:*

> The plains are afloat in mysterious space, and the winds come straight from heaven. Anyone alone in the plains turns into a mystic. . . . Something happens to a man when he gets on a horse, in a country where he can ride at a run forever; it is quite easy to ascend to an impression of living in a myth. He either feels like a god or feels closer to God.

(I would extend these remarks to apply to women as well and to include motion of any kind across the plains, even by automobile.)

While I might resist being tagged a mystic, I do agree generally with this description of the effect of the plains on the psyche. Many of my poems are about unrestrained motion across the land and the convictions and perceptions that rise from that motion. And on the plains, it seems easy to believe any single life is part of a larger pattern, part of a deified pattern. All life—whether blue gamma and buffalo grasses, or killdeer, horned lark, forbs or foxes, the white-tailed jack rabbit, purple prairie gentians, fireflies, tumble bugs—all life of the plains is encompassed and carried beyond itself in significance, even as each individual retains its own unique being.

Whether one feels lost or empowered on those very great Great Plains, freedom is a conviction inherent to those spaces, not just physical freedom or freedom of motion, but an untethered, windswept freedom of the imagination and possibility. I believe in the virtue of this kind of open freedom in writing. I maintain a commitment to this freedom, so easy to apprehend on the plains, and to the energy and affirmation that rise from it.

(1999)

( PART II )

# This Nature

Bach is nature, and the Marquis de Sade is nature. Florence Nightingale and the Iron Maiden are nature. Michelangelo's *Pietà*, the swastika, *Penthouse* magazine, and solar flares are nature. Pedophiles and saints equally are nature. Ash pits, boggy graves, nuclear bombs, *tubercle bacillus*, Yosemite Falls, abortion, the polio vaccine, all are part of the sum total of everything that is and therefore nature. Nothing that is goes against nature, because nature is the way things are. Nature is what is, everything that is, everything that has been, and everything that is possible, including human actions, inventions, creations, and imaginations. This is my definition. This nature is the nature of roaches and cheetahs and honeysuckle, the nature of a Strauss waltz, the nature of the Ice Ages, the bubonic plague, the eruption of Krakatoa, the nature of the slaughter of American bison, the nature of human sacrifice and bloody rituals carried out by Aztecs, Celts, Slavs.

Nothing that exists, including language, is outside nature. We do not know an "outside nature," because knowledge itself is an element of nature. Even the word "unnatural" is part of nature (how could it otherwise be here on this page?) and is therefore self-contradictory.

An ice pick through the chest or a soothing hand on the forehead, both are natural, both gestures of nature. Wild curly dock, malaria, exploding stars, continental drift, and the construction of Hoover Dam are natural, part of what is. Violent birth and violent extinction are older than we are and natural. We know a history of both. We have sometimes been involved in the nature of both. We cannot legitimately use the word "natural" as synonymous with the words "unsullied," "pure," or "righteous."

It is no more against nature for human beings to clear-cut a forest than it is against nature for Mt. Vesuvius to erupt and eliminate the town of Herculaneum. Human actions may be judged moral or immoral, wise or unwise, cruel or benevolent, heedless or thoughtful, but those are other terms and other issues. I am speaking of nature. Everything that we name noble is nature, and everything we name despicable is nature, and our attempt to distinguish between the noble and the despicable is nature.

Calculus, astrophysics, the automobile, the safety pin, and billboards were created by creatures born of the natural world and thus included naturally in the nature of everything that is. If we create justice, it exists in nature. If we act so as to bring compassion into existence, it is real within the natural world. Divinity is of the universe, part of nature, when it is observed and noted and imagined and expressed by creatures born of nature with physical, blood-beating, light-snapping minds. We are thoroughly nature. To claim otherwise is to attempt to place human beings and every-thing we do in some rare, unimaginable realm beyond the universe, thus rendering the power of our origins lost and our obligations vague.

Nature is everything that is. We are not and cannot be "unnatural." Our choices and our actions are never for or against nature. They are always simply of nature. Our decisions then involve determining what it is that we value among this everything-that-is, this nature. What is it we seek to preserve? to eliminate? to modify? to accept? to avoid? to cherish? to respect? to emulate? The decisions we make, how we justify and construct those decisions and the behavior that results, all these become part of the great milieu, and they have their effects in ways we may not always recognize. Our choices and our actions, whether based on aesthetic considerations, moral or spiritual con-siderations, economic considerations, or rational consid-erations, must be justified in some way other than by the claim that they are in accord with the natural world; for any behavior, even murder, even suicide, even war, even abuse of the young, can be justified by that claim. We may call these particular acts horrors, but they are horrors that are part of nature, part of everything that is, and they cannot be said to go against nature. They are horrors that are part of nature already replete with horrors. Perhaps these particular acts go against our sense of goodness or compassion, moral-ity or beauty or justice, but they do not go against nature.

Annihilation and creation are occurring constantly around us now, and they have occurred always, long before human beings came to be. Nature encompasses all contradictions.

This nature is not a single entity, not a consistent force that sanctions or condemns behavior, not a god-substitute that we can embrace or blame or escape. It comprises the entire, complex myriad of ever-changing events and details, unpredictable, paradoxical, passing and eternal, known and mysterious. Nature is the vast expanse of abstractions and multiplicities; it is the void and the concrete presence, an unrestricted inclusiveness. The definition of the word "nature" even includes its own definition and the maker of its definition. It is self-referential.

I deliberately seek out the specific aspects of everything that is that I find ennobling, affirming, that engender in me hope, faith, action, and health, the chaos and mystery that energizes me. I select and cling to them. I choose to value and praise them. Just a few of these aspects, for me, are the words of Shakespeare, Dostoyevsky, Whitman, Melville, Twain, Faulkner, Roethke, Jesus Christ; the music of Chopin, Beethoven, Bruckner, Anne-Sophie Mutter, the Takács Quartet; the very existence of the body of preserved art, music, and literature that is my culture; the Magna Carta, the Constitution of the United States, and the Bill of Rights; arches, domes, and columns; the grace and order of an NBA basketball game; Jeremy Brett as Sherlock Holmes; the curiosity, facility, and complexity of the human mind that results in the revelations of science; the way sunlight appears—shifting its illuminations and colors on roofs and gardens and fields, making shadows of trees on the curtains—through the gradual coming of morning, throughout the patterns of evening, everyday, the gift of morning and evening; snow, that amazement; the surrounding great buffer of stars in which we are immersed; life in its unrelenting, ruthless, self-absorbed, tenacious grasp on being.

We are fortunate as human beings to have the opportunity to discern and to act, to recognize and experience ourselves in this welter of terror and beauty, to add our praise, gratitude, and testimony to the totality of everything that is, to place them, as if we were placing seeds into soil, into the flux and form of this nature.

(1999)

# Small and Insignificant,
# Mighty and Glorious

Across the street from the elementary school I attended in the late 1940s stood a very small grocery store maintained by an elderly man and his wife. Each wore identical, long, white aprons with bibs and string ties that circled their waists and knotted over their abundant stomachs. The store had a worn, wooden floor that creaked in a welcoming way when anyone entered. Didn't all small, family-owned grocery stores of the 1940s have such floors? I remember them that way. The light inside the store was dim, but not so dim that I and my friends couldn't clearly see the various penny candies displayed inside their glass case. The store smelled of strawberry and banana taffy. Sometimes I had a nickel to spend after lunch. That was heavenly.

Every spring a young man would appear, as if dropped from the sky, on the porch of this store. He was a slight man with a darker skin than mine, from Manila, so we were told, and he wore a colorful, tropical shirt, nothing like the shirts my dad wore. This intriguing man sold yo-yos, and he was a genuine expert with the toy. Up and down his yo-yo would wheel, spinning fast, between his legs and over his head and, spinning still, roll along on the sidewalk in a trick called "walking the dog" until it was jerked back up its string to be caught perfectly in his hand. It was awesome to watch.

The fortunate child who purchased a yo-yo received not only this wooden toy shiny with fluorescent colors, just like the yo-yo that performed such marvelous feats, but also, free of charge, a scene carved on its side by this man from Manila, carved with a small pen knife right before the child's eyes. The carving depicted a scene from his native land—palm trees and mountains, sometimes a stream, a hut, sometimes even the owner's name. The child who possessed such a yo-yo could always admire the scene, running a finger over the lines of it, even if the particular yo-yo never behaved, tangling and twisting at the end-length of its string.

Would it be proper to label this master of yo-yo skills, talented also at carving landscapes on his wooden wares, an *artist*? Probably not. Did his talents, performed on the porch of a small grocery store in a small Midwestern town, constitute a spiritual experience? Few would call it so. But suppose a painter replicated that scene taking place at lunchtime on an early April day, suggested with oils on canvas the delight and adoration on the faces of the boys and girls gathered around, the pleasure the man took perhaps in his skill, perhaps in the rapt attention of the children, perhaps in the colors and sounds of the spring day with its new sun, perhaps in the all-in-all. Or suppose the scene was described in a cadence of language, with words that evoked the vitality, the unique camaraderie and complex interaction between humans and the details of this place and time. Or suppose the patterns and rhythms existing among the children and the man and the yo-yos, the warming earth, the storekeepers watching from the doorway, the motions and sounds of returning birds, were expressed by violins, flutes, oboes, clarinets, timpani. Suppose through their works the painter, the poet, the composer, the musicians conveyed both the loss of this moment and the eternal nature of this moment. This we might call art. This we might call spiritual.

The arts are those disciplines that bring to our awareness our deepest and most persistent yearnings, longings that are always present with us to a lesser or greater extent. The arts, in their various manifestations, remind us of these basic and profound yearnings, whether the yearning concerns our inability to define ourselves, or our inability to reconcile the inner contradictions of our being, or our inability to grasp the essence of the physical world, or whether the yearning is for life everlasting, or for a union with that which we occasionally perceive as eternal and divine, or for release from grief or fear or ignorance, or a yearning for peace or love or for an understanding of how to celebrate and praise adequately. I would classify all of these as aspects of the yearning for the spiritual, and I would define art as revealing these yearnings in original, evocative, and insightful ways.

The arts do not resolve or fulfill our yearnings for the spiritual. They offer no answers. They may evoke our yearning; they may heighten and delineate it, thereby enabling us to recall it, but they will not relieve it for long. The arts do not indoctrinate. Their interpretations of spiritual yearning are often contradictory. They display a multiplicity of human experiences within the parameters that each work establishes for itself. Our finest artists are those whose works have endured and touched the hearts of many people of different generations and times with their portrayals of spiritual seeking and spiritual confusion. The arts investigate our longings and the source of our longings in stories, dramas and poetry, in sculpture and paintings, through music and dance, in architecture, through careful observation and investigation of the physical universe. In this last respect, I am including science in my definition of the arts, because the essence of science is an expression of the yearning to understand the ways of the physical world.

In *The Structure of Evolutionary Theory*, Stephen Jay Gould expresses one aspect of spiritual insight that results from scientific investigation: "Something almost unspeakably holy—I don't know how else to say this—underlies our discovery and confirmation of the actual details that made our world and also, in realms of contingency, assured the minutiae of its construction in the manner we know, and not in any one of a trillion other ways, nearly all of which would not have included the evolution of a scribe to record the beauty, the cruelty, the fascination, and the mystery." The art of science is to reveal and address our yearning to understand the universe around us, the yearning inherent to our curiosity about the immediate reality we witness.

I propose a trinity composed of the physical universe,

spirituality, and art. These three are one, I believe, each needing the others in order to exist, each influencing and contributing to the others.

Spirituality resides in the physical world and depends upon it. Where else would spirituality reside but in the concrete, in that which we encounter through the senses? Where else but in the hand of a man carving a picture for a child on a wooden toy, in children gathered around a porch on a spring day, in the call of an unseen bird in a tree above them, in the complex interweaving of all their shadows with the light of the sun?

And the physical universe depends on the arts to discover and bring into being its more subtle and elusive spiritual nature.

And the arts require both the material of the physical universe and its latent spirituality. Where else would the arts go for their themes, their metaphors, their rhythms and patterns, their energy, their paradoxes, but to the structures and shapes, the hard stuff of the tangible that is the source of their work and their life?

What is a high wind without the exaltation of a paper kite dipping and fluttering, crackling in the sky? What are the wind and the kite without an artistic expression of this exaltation? Spirituality compensates for the ephemeral nature of the physical universe, as the physical universe provides place for the spiritual. It is an ancient human wish that the word become flesh, that the spiritual be recognized in the flesh. The arts address this wish. The physical universe, spirituality, and art are inextricably bound together and dependent upon one another for their existence and the totality of their possibilities.

It is true that we do not live by bread alone. There is an aspect of our being that requires spiritual nourishment. But it is also true that we require bread to live. Because bread can satisfy our physical hunger, it has become a symbol in many of the arts for the satisfaction of spiritual hunger. Bread serves as a symbol of well-being, gratitude, and offering. Individuals declare their unity as a community symbolically by the breaking of bread together, the sharing of bread. The body of Christ is described as an offering broken as bread is broken and satisfying spiritual hunger as bread satisfies our physical hunger. Within the physical body of bread resides its spiritual dimension realized through techniques common to the arts: symbolism and metaphor. The functioning trinity of art, the physical world, and spirituality is evident here.

Alfred North Whitehead in *Science and Religion* states: "Religion is the vision of something which stands beyond, behind and within the passing flux of immediate things; something which is real, and yet waiting to be realised; . . . something that gives meaning to all that passes and yet eludes apprehension."

I believe "religion" and "spirituality" are synonymous within the context of this statement. It is the discipline of the arts that endeavors to realize that elusive vision within the "passing flux" of the physical world, the vision of which Whitehead speaks. The arts attempt to portray this vision through our yearning for it.

The artistry of a guitarist and a human voice can realize the spiritual peace of a slow-moving river. The written word can evoke the freedom a river suggests or portray the water of a river as a medium for spiritual cleansing. A choir, an orchestra, and Beethoven remind us of brotherhood and the joy of living. *Romeo and Juliet*, through Shakespeare's drama and Prokofiev's music, each in its separate ways, elucidates the exhilaration of passionate love. The visual arts can depict for us the face of fear, halting a moment of death, halting a moment of war so that we may feel with all of our faculties its destructive power and horror and so reinforce our determination to encourage peace. Van Gogh reveals through the art of orange and golden oils the affirmation of spirituality in sunflowers in a vase.

In "The Lace Maker," Carl Dennis writes of Vermeer's portrait of a woman creating art with needle and thread:

So Vermeer
Offers a silent tribute to another artist

Who's increasing the number of beautiful
Useless things available in a world
That would be darker and smaller without them.

We need beauty, we need the affirmation of beauty, we need the spirituality of beauty found within the physical world in order to live, to be vibrant, healthy, and generous people. Our ability to respond to our spiritual needs depends in part on our ability to recognize those needs. The finest of the arts reveal to us those needs in the sharpest, most distinct, most penetrating evocations and, in so doing, enlarge and brighten the world.

A character in "The Deluge at Norderney," from Isak Dinesen's *Seven Gothic Tales*, puts forward the thought that ". . . while the book of the Father is given in the Old Testament, and that of the Son, in the New, the testament of the Third Person of the Trinity still remained to be written." I believe the testament of the spirit will never be a completed testament, hopefully never finished, hopefully never codified. Instead the testament of the spirit is an ongoing testament created continuously by artists of every discipline and every time.

My older brother owned a gorgeous, pearlescent yo-yo bought from the man from Manila and complete with a carving of that strange, faraway place. Both are lost somewhere now, yo-yo and man, lost but retained. I, the little sister, admired that yo-yo, and I admired my brother for having the courage to speak to this man, to sit beside him on the cement steps of the store as he carved that scene, so foreign, almost otherworldly to a seven-year-old girl living in Missouri. I have recalled here the yo-yo, the yo-yo master, and the aura of their time with joy and with nostalgia and with knowledge of the spiritual potential inherent to each, the same spiritual potential inherent to all lives and features, small and insignificant, mighty and glorious, of the physical world.

(2002)

# What among Heavens and Suns

*(The following is the written version of remarks given at the 1996 John Hay Award colloquium honoring Ann Zwinger and her work, March 10, 1996, in Colorado Springs, Colorado. The weekend focused on discussions of the desire to write and what experiences and beliefs sustain that work. These remarks were delivered outside in the mountains, on the final day of the colloquium.)*

When we gather together, questions of why we write and who we perceive our audience to be repeat themselves—causing each of us to reiterate the basic impulse behind our writing and to realize again how often we must go back to that source. Why write? Flannery O'Connor said, "I write because I'm good at it." There's a level of truth in that. But we all know it's more than that too.

Most of my poems begin when something captures my attention—a phrase, a word, a sound, a branch of red berries against the sky, the way a killdeer flies up before me. For some reason I'm captured by that, enchanted, curious. Wanting to understand *why* I am so captured is where the poem starts. I begin by asking questions, allowing the music of the language to answer, to lead me by its sounds and cadences. If something gets down on the page and my body feels excited by it and I'm pleased, I continue to go in that direction. If I'm bored, if the language is dull, plodding, expected, lacking surprise, no matter how clear or accurate, I turn another way.

Ron Carlson, a fiction writer, compares the process of writing a short story to the experience of being lost in the woods, searching for his way. He doesn't begin knowing precisely what the plot will be or what perceptions will emerge. The process of writing the story involves discoveries made as the language comes into being and finds the way.

Often we come to our writing in distress over environmental concerns, wishing to articulate the details of those concerns, to alert others. But when the aim of our writing is advocacy, when we intend to give a message, we begin writing already knowing what that message is. We are not lost in the woods, not feeling our way, exploring with language, hoping to illuminate a blindness of our own. We are not open to the unexpected. We know already where we're going and where we want to end; there may be a little surprise along the way; but the route is mapped out. As a result, the language usually lacks vibrancy and originality. As Robert Frost put it, "No surprise for the writer, no surprise for the reader."

The audience we imagine for our writing also influences what gets written. Is our audience a perceived adversary, one we wish to accuse or to win to our convictions? Or is the audience an editor we admire? Do we write to a lover, or to the best part of ourselves—that part of ourselves that we wish we were all the time? Is the audience God? Whether we articulate it or not, we envision the receiver of our writing, and that receiver will influence the voice we adopt and the language we choose. Is the receiver one who will broaden all possibilities of the writing or will the conceived audience limit the imagination, limit the possible discoveries?

We know there is an art to good writing—those skills we practice in order to gain ease with the language, the language becoming one with the body, as a musical instrument becomes an extension of the body of an excellent musician. The finest literature is the art of exploration, using language as a tool of the body, letting the imagination play. Whatever restricts that exploration—the breadth of discovery—should be left out of the process.

If the writing is relaying an actual, personal experience in the physical world—what is the role of the imagination? The following passage, translated by Ivan Morris from *The Pillow Book* written in the tenth century by Sei Shonagon, a handmaiden to the empress of Japan, reflects a common problem:

> I remember a clear morning in the Ninth Month when it had been raining all night. Despite the bright sun, dew was still dripping from the chrysanthemums in the garden. On the bamboo fences and crisscross hedges I saw tatters of spider webs; and where the threads were broken the raindrops hung on them like strings of white pearls. I was greatly moved and delighted.
>
> As it became sunnier, the dew gradually vanished from

the clover and the other plants where it had lain so heavily;
the branches began to stir, then suddenly sprang up of their
own accord. Later I described to people how beautiful it
all was. What most impressed me was that they were not at
all impressed.

Shonagon was observant and precise in her language. Yet
even though she had given a lovely description of this scene,
capturing it in the finest detail, it hadn't touched others. But
the best writing always moves beyond mere description to an
insight or a surprising turn, as Shonagon's does in her last
line. If our aim is to write the very finest literature—literature that we hope can speak to people, as most of Shonagon's
recollections do, nine hundred years from now—then we
must go beyond the merely realistic re-creation of the natural world. If we want our writing to speak to universal concerns, then we must ask deeper questions.

We live in a scientific age in which the questions asked of
nature are mostly those that science is best suited to answer.
But maybe nature gives answers in response to the *kinds* of
questions we ask. What questions could we ask of nature
that relate to the spirit, how to deal with grief, for example,
or to the place of love in the processes of the physical
world? What crucial questions have not yet been formulated? Part of our task as writers is to take imaginative risks
in formulating questions that will allow nature to respond
beyond the arena of science, while still in accord with the
responses science has received, those questions that might
expose aspects of the universe not yet perceived.

Sometimes I think, how could it have happened that evolution led to a creature who suddenly stopped, turned around, looked this world straight on, and asked, "What is this? Who am I?" What are we doing on this wondrous orb that seems to be turning, moving around an ordinary star in the deep blackness, surrounded by this confusion and explosion of racing multitudes of fiery gases? One day I looked at the sun and thought, What is that great big frightening thing up there? It's so hot and bright, almost roaring, and we have to squint our eyes to look at it, every day overwhelmingly stunning in its blazing. We write in order to remember the remarkable in the commonplace, the wonder of the inexplicable, even in the smallest phenomenon, even in the rainbow grasshopper, even in the mite of the splendid tiger beetle.

We are pretty ignorant creatures, really. Our brains just don't work very well. We hardly have control over them. A memory, some scrap of word or image, will suddenly flash through—not anything that you would even consider significant in your life. But all of a sudden it's there, and then it disappears. Part of being a writer is developing the ability to grab those things that go rushing through, getting them down somewhere until there is time to go back and consider whether they are nonsense or important. Some will be keys.

I was educated to believe that the universal human condition is what all great literature addresses—those concerns that don't disappear with time, the common dilemmas, heartaches, joys, and bewilderments that all humans have experienced. And this business of who we are and how we got here always leads me to remember that all of this is a gift—this life, our surroundings. We did absolutely nothing to earn it. We didn't do anything to earn the rattlebox cry of a magpie, or the flickering notes of a wind through aspens, or the fragrance of a pine . . . (*coyote howls heard in the distance*) . . . coyotes? Well, we did nothing to earn that either. All these gifts were given to us at the moment of our births. So the question rises: What do we give back in gratitude? That is one reason for writing. And the question that rises next is, if all of this is a gift, everything that we enjoy, all the beauty, and even the horror that keeps us alert and attentive, then who is the giver? Who or what is the benevolence that not only gave us all this to experience but gave us the ability to question it?

There's no easy answer, and there's probably no single answer. But it seems to me that the effort to touch this benevolence in our work—whether you call it God, divinity, spirituality—to attempt to come closer to it with language, is another aim of the writing. It's a task that all generations, all ages, all cultures have engaged.

We have an obligation. We must produce for our time the finest, the best, the clearest, the most imaginative and beautiful literature that we can, using all of the ability and talent and past knowledge we can draw on. We must do this so that a record of what our time was like, what caused us sorrow, what we rejoiced in, how we tried to learn ways of conducting ourselves that were beneficial and not destructive, so that those who come after us may know that in our efforts we experienced conflicts and failed often. We must create a literature that reveals that even with all our failures, all our weaknesses, in our ignorance and with an incomplete language, we struggled to articulate our concerns and dilemmas, to celebrate adequately, to understand how to negotiate gracefully in a world of beauty and terror.

(1996)

# Twentieth-Century Cosmology
## and the Soul's Habitation

I'm very curious about the grid upon which we place our-selves in our minds in time and space. There must be a grid of some kind there for each of us, a visual scaffolding, for balance, for orientation. Where and how do we envision ourselves located in time and space? born in a certain year? at a certain location? by calendar? by map?

But is there more than that in our vision? Do we estab-lish shapes and patterns that form boundaries of history and place inside of which we see ourselves and by which we define ourselves? Do we have an underlying conception of our spatial location in the world when we are out walking or traveling by air, inside our homes, here and now? What exactly is the "here and now" for our culture? And does this placing of ourselves in the universe affect our structure of moral values, the way we order our experiences, the way we explain our origins to ourselves? They must be related. What does it mean to our image of family, landscape, art, to believe that light travels at a constant speed, that light falling through the forest at this moment left the surface of the sun nine minutes before or that looking up into the stars we are seeing back through billions of years? What a strange conception—that light carries not only knowledge but time and distance as well.

What exactly is our cosmology then, the cosmology of our culture today, and how much does it affect our thinking? Does our cosmology permeate the language in subtle ways, the language then structuring our perceptions? These are questions of interest to me, and I don't have the answers to them. I'd like to hear other opinions.

I'm going to define cosmology as the story of the universe, the explanation of the origin and history and processes of the universe, an explanation that creates the structure upon which we locate ourselves and define ourselves in relation to the objects we observe around us, and by which we also address our own origins and our nature.

Edward R. Harrison, in *Cosmology: The Science of the Universe*, states the importance of cosmology in this way: "Every society creates universes, and not only do these universes reflect the societies, but each universe controls the history and destiny of its society. The most powerful and influential ideas in any society are those that relate to the universe; they shape history, inspire civilizations, foment wars, create empires and establish political systems."

Previous cultures have invented a variety of cosmologies. Some have told stories of magic, stories that explained everything by the motives and actions of ambient spirits inhabiting the natural world and fashioned in the image of mankind. The cosmology of mythology constructed a universe in which the spirits of magic retreated and became remote gods. Anthropocentric cosmologies pictured human beings at the center of the universe, above the beasts, occupying a place of importance, next to the angels, possessing the attention of the creator of all things. During the Middle Ages, cosmology and religion were one.

But according to Harrison, "No persons living in the twentieth century can claim to be educated if they are unaware of the modern vision of the physical universe and the history of the magnificent concepts that it embodies."

I do believe that the cosmology of our times is at the root of much of what we write and the attitudes and values we espouse, whether we are completely aware of it or not. The world picture we hold today has for the most part been given to us by science, and all of us believe it, to some degree, and even more importantly, whether we declare we believe in it or not, we act on it, base decisions on it, live by it, and demonstrate daily our faith in it.

Now I just want to state very briefly and simply the way I believe many of us visualize the universe and our place in it, the way I, as a lay person, understand our cosmology. Most of us are so accustomed to these ideas that they may seem ordinary and unsurprising, which proves my contention that this is the cosmology of our time, held closely by the members of our community.

We see ourselves as very tiny beings made up physically of groupings of other even tinier entities, atoms, molecules, cells, and organs. We are made from the dust of old stars. Most of us believe we have risen through natural selection and mutation of genes over many, many millions of years, our bodies being related to all other living bodies on the earth. Beautiful and fine, lovely story, invigorating and incorporating theory in my opinion.

And we see ourselves as very tiny beings relative to the size of the earth, our planet, third from the sun in a family of eight planets all circling the sun, the star closest to us. We understand our earth is tiny compared to the size of our star (I remember being taught as a child that the size of the earth compared to the size of the sun was as a pea relative to a basketball). The sun is 740 times more massive than the eight major planets together.

The sun is tiny compared to the size of the solar system, the solar system to the size of the Milky Way Galaxy, the Milky Way Galaxy to the size of the Andromeda Galaxy, which is twice as big, containing four hundred billion stars. And yet the Andromeda Galaxy is tiny compared to the universe, containing many billions of other galaxies. All of that, up there, going on at this moment.

This, very sketchily, is the way I perceive the structure of our location within the universe, where we place ourselves in the organization of the celestial objects we recognize around us. On the surface of the earth, we visualize and state our location conventionally by imaginary coordinates, latitude and longitude, by North Pole and South Pole, by hemisphere, by relation to the ocean upon which we sail or beside which we live or the mountain range to the east or to the west, by the geographical and political boundaries of our community. If we say "Montana," most of us can visualize the shape and place of that entity on the globe

(North Pole at the top), the same with Puget Sound or the Mississippi River or the Panama Canal.

We visualize the shape of the earth and its continents by the maps and photographs we've been shown, some taken from space, geographical maps, geological maps, computer-generated three-dimensional maps, heat-generated maps recorded by satellite. If you imagine at this moment where you are on the globe, something visual must occur. This picture comes to us through science and technology.

We believe, so our story goes, that we are being carried on this spinning Earth that turns on its own axis at a speed so fast we can't even feel it. Our Earth, bearing with it one orbiting moon, then circles and tilts around the sun, which is borne along itself with the solar system on its path around the center of the Milky Way, the Milky Way and its billions of sun/stars moving as one body, where? Simply away from all other cosmic bodies, a result of the Big Bang theory of the origin of the universe as we currently understand it. We aren't really sitting still at all, but are caught up in this mayhem of motion.

We perceive the time span of our existence, even as a species, as fleeting compared to the life span of some now extinct species (dinosaurs, for example), and we have figures to prove this aspect of our insignificance. Our lives are fleeting compared to the age of the earth, the history of the sun, the solar system, the Milky Way, a pulsar, a quasar. . . .

The story our cosmology tells is that we exist in a universe of flux, not only the rushing river that can never be stepped in twice, but stars in the process of being born and dying, our own sun in decline, expending itself. (Could anyone come across an article entitled "The Death of the Sun," as I did recently, and not feel a sudden fear and stillness in his heart?) The mountains that once seemed so sure and enduring to other generations in their cosmologies, we know now they too have risen and will wear away. Floors of the ocean and platforms under the continents shift and slowly collide, greatly altering the surface of the earth. Forests grow up and fall away. Oceans enlarge and decline. Ice sheets form, descend, and retreat. Volcanoes, like Krakatoa, erupt, alter the climate, and affect life on Earth for centuries. Strong, successful species gain ascendancy on the earth, then eventually wane and vanish. Civilizations full of vibrant and brilliant minds come and go. Our own bodies, the cells of our brains, finely balanced, die and replace themselves constantly.

We also understand our physical being as the result of very slow, apparently random changes, mutations occurring within the DNA, the hereditary code, gradual transformations and adaptations that took place over a very long period of time. We can witness adaptive evolutionary changes in some animals (insects, small fish, some birds and amphibians) during our own lifetimes. We have watched our own civilization change and alter the earth, eradicate certain diseases, create bacteria, manipulate the development of domesticated animals, affect the environment.

Flux and change are constant, so the story goes.

If human consciousness should play a role in the well-being of the universe, we aren't certain what that role is. Our cosmology seems not to directly address this issue.

If there is a power or a creator interested in us (though I think the doubt many of us feel in this regard is so deep and pervasive that the issue is hardly mentioned anymore, at least not in the same breath as our cosmology), we aren't certain in what way that power might manifest itself or what vocabulary is suitable for addressing its existence.

As a result of this cosmology, all of us, I would venture to say, have seen ourselves, at some moment or another, as "mankind cast aimlessly adrift in a meaningless universe" (Harrison). To further complicate the story—we have experienced in the twentieth century a sudden and continual influx into our culture of massive amounts of information, information that affects the story our cosmology tells, new information published constantly concerning the heavens and the evolutionary processes of stars, the discovery of new elementary particles, information redefining time, detailed and profuse information on the processes by which animal and plant species function and survive, information about the geological history of the earth and extinct species, information about other human cultures past and present, about the human body, the human brain, the human psyche, information about new technologies that radically alter forms of communication, vigorous exploration of both the very large and the microscopic, even invisible neutrinos, books and books on just the history of the violin, for instance, the history of bread, the history of locks and keys, the history of paperweights, for heaven's sake. You name it and at least one person has written a book about it, with many more, we are certain, to come.

I chose at random one page from the *Oxford-Duden*

*Pictorial English Dictionary*, a dictionary that lists some 28,000 objects from a whole range of technical activities and everyday situations. Listed on this one page are 103 terms dealing simply with roofs and roofing.

I don't believe any previous culture has ever had such a massive vocabulary available to it as does ours today. Every word, every word, I believe, a possible metaphor.

All these oceans of information can be daunting enough, but add to that the fact that much of this information is changing and refining itself continually—and the result is often despair. One is almost fearful to utter a declarative sentence unless its implications are so narrow and qualified—i.e., "This is how I myself personally think I myself alone might possibly have felt just a moment ago maybe"— that it becomes inane.

So, like the universe, we conceive of our cosmology as constantly changing, altering itself too according to new data, more refined methods of gathering information. We are reluctant then to put our wholehearted faith in all the details of this story, the cosmology as it is constructed today.

This is a very strange and unique facet of our cosmology, that it instructs us not to allow ourselves to fully believe it as it is told today. We must reserve the right always to critically review the cosmology. The cosmology itself tells us this. This is one of its own characteristics, part of its very own tenets and story—its request for suspension of full commitment, its own insistence on a critical eye and mind at work on itself.

This is very, very different from the cosmologies of past

cultures. Our cosmology tells us we must be willing to accept new, corroborated information that may dismiss or alter parts of its story as previously related. The story adjusts and expands. Rigidity is definitely not a part of our cosmology. Science is not rigid. Dogmas are rigid.

So maybe we like this cosmology, the excitement and astonishment of its grand ideas, the vastness and power and mystery of the universe it describes, the beauty of its intricacies, the freedom of thought it affords. Maybe we love the very fact of its openness, its willingness to adapt itself, its willingness actually to respond to us. That is pretty fine and wonderful, I think.

Or maybe we don't like this cosmology. We might be willing and eager to ascribe to seeing a universe in a grain of sand but a changing universe in every grain of sand! at every moment! And at times our cosmology seems to describe a universe that takes no cognizance of us, to describe a universe indifferent to us, "a world of quantity, of reified geometry, a world in which, though there is a place for everything, there is no place for man" as described by A. Koyre in *Newtonian Studies*. Maybe this is the source of much literature of despair or a literature seeking consolation, the literature of seeking consolation in the natural world on Earth. Maybe.

And if we had been given a choice, perhaps we would have created a different cosmology. I'm not arguing that this cosmology is right or wrong, complete or incomplete, eternal or ephemeral, satisfying or disturbing. But I am saying this cosmology is the one that is ours. Not only does it provide much of the vocabulary and many of the images of our time, but the way we live and survive physically depends on it. It is integral to our daily lives.

Simply walking out into a wilderness and leaving behind temporarily the life, the accoutrements of our human communities, doesn't mean we leave behind this cosmology. It's part of our being. We carry it with us right out onto the tundra, into the rainforest, diving beneath the ocean. In fact, we understand these very designations of *tundra, rainforest, ocean* in part by the light of our cosmology.

The effect of the vision created by our cosmology is evident in a description by Richard Nelson when he writes of the experience of surfing in Alaska, in his book *The Island Within*.

> Shortly, an even larger series of swells approaches, but I'm far enough out to catch the biggest one and prudent enough to make it my last. As I wade ashore, I watch the energy of the wave die, rushing to the top of the beach and slipping back down again. And I remember its power rising to a crescendo around and under me during the final moments of its life, after traversing a thousand miles of ocean from its birthplace in a far Pacific storm. The motion that so exalted me was given freely by the wave, as the wave was given motion by the wind, as the wind was given motion by the storm, as the storm was given motion by the whirl of the atmosphere and the turning of the earth itself. Then I remember the sea lions, cradled by the same ocean and pleasured by the same waves. All of us here, partaking of a single motion. Together and alive.

And again Barry Lopez, in "Offshore: A Journey to the Weddell Sea," eloquently describes this vision on board the

*Nataniel B. Palmer,* an ice-breaking scientific research vessel, as
it heads for the southern seas.

> The bridge, its wings cantilevered over ship and ocean on
> either side and its vast ability to communicate and to navi-
> gate so implicit in its mute antennas, nearly fills one's field
> of vision. Above it and beyond tonight is the blackest blue
> sky riven cleanly by the familiar tingling spine of suns,
> the Galaxy seen edge-on. Watching the bridge move under
> the stars, feeling the ship's engines thrum in my legs, and
> standing in a breeze high above the ocean's smooth, dark
> plain—and then sensing the plunging depth, the shadowed
> plain of the Peru Basin below, the complex signal codes of
> the bioluminescence winking there above the basin floor like
> stars—I thought, this must be sailing.

This vision of place and relationships, this cosmology,
is our myth. We carry it with us in our memories, in our
gestures, our bones, just as we carry *Hamlet* or the music of
Bach or the Christmas story or the vision of our bedroom
at home or the act of turning a page in a book or the face
of our mother. There's no getting rid of it. No hope of that.

So what do the underlying concepts of this cosmology
that we carry with us do to language? We know our language
has been greatly enhanced and enlarged simply through the
vocabulary given us by the sciences. We know that much.
How do the images presented us through this cosmology,
the vision of planets moving in their orbits through space,
the solar system intersected by comets and asteroids, for
example, affect the frameworks and metaphors upon which
we construct our literature? How does the cosmology affect

our choices of subject matter, the tone, confident or abject, in the first line of the poem or essay, our stance toward the hour of the day, the way we regard a rookery of sea lions, eagles clasping claws mid-air, the arrow-straight morning sun through the window, across the sheets?

I've already suggested that this cosmology may be the source of much of today's literature of despair, or literature that turns inward, becomes solipsistic, literature seeking consolation in some kind of certainty that is perceived as being absent from our cosmology. But are there effects much more subtle?

And even more crucial, how does our cosmology influence our definitions of loyalty, honesty, dignity, art, love?

We can be sure the effects are there, and in order to develop the strongest beliefs possible, beliefs that enable us to act with conviction, dignity, and generosity, we must understand, recognize, and acknowledge the story of our cosmology, which is shaping the attitudes we take toward ourselves and our world, and also our conceptions of our potentialities. We must learn how to grasp our cosmology fully and to infuse it with a sustaining spirituality. A statement by Bertrand Russell in "A Free Man's Worship" from his book *Mysticism and Logic* succinctly defines the despair that can rise from our cosmology.

> That man is the product of causes which had no prevision
> of the end they were achieving; that his origin, his growth,
> his hopes and fears, his loves and his beliefs, are but the
> outcome of accidental collocations of atoms; that no fire, no
> heroism, no intensity of thought or feeling, can preserve a

life beyond the grave; that all the labors of the ages, all the devotion, all the inspirations, all the noonday brightness of human genius, are destined to extinction in the vast death of the solar system; and the whole temple of Man's achievement must inevitably be buried beneath the debris of a universe in ruins—all these things, if not quite beyond dispute, are yet so nearly certain, that no philosophy which rejects them can hope to stand. Only within the scaffolding of these truths, only on the firm foundation of unyielding despair, can the soul's habitation be safely built.

The point of departure must be "unyielding despair." We start from the recognition of that point to build the soul's habitation.

Beginning there, we should understand that science is in the business of measuring things. The model of the universe, the cosmology that science creates, is based on what science is able to measure. It is the fallacy of misplaced concreteness then to proclaim that this model is the total reality. The model is not untrue, but only partial, not all-inclusive. If this model were complete, and scientists believed it to be complete, the business of science would come to an abrupt halt. Total truth has not yet been discovered.

Jacob Bronowski, in his book *The Origin of Knowledge and Imagination*, describes another limitation on any investigation of the universe.

I believe that the world is totally connected: that is to say, that there are no events anywhere in the universe which are not tied to every other event in the universe. I regard this to some extent as a metaphysical statement, although you

will see, as I develop it in the next lecture, it has a much
more down-to-earth content than that. But I will repeat it:
I believe that every event in the world is connected to every
other event. But you cannot carry on science on the supposition that you are going to be able to connect every event
with every other event. . . . It is, therefore, an essential part
of the methodology of science to divide the world for any
experiment into what we regard as relevant and what we
regard, for purposes of that experiment, as irrelevant.

We make a cut. We put the experiment, if you like, into
a box. Now the moment we do that, we do violence to the
connections in the world. We may have the best cause in the
world. I may say, "Well, come on, I am not really going to
think that the light from Sirius is going to affect the reading
of this micrometer!" And I say this although I can see Sirius
clearly with the naked eye, and I have the impertinence to
say that though the light of Sirius affects my rods and cones
it is not going to affect the experiment. Therefore we have
always, if I may use another Talmudic phrase, to put a fence
round the law, to put a fence round the law of nature that we
are trying to tease out. And we have to say, "For purposes of
this experiment everything outside here is regarded as irrelevant, and everything inside here is regarded as relevant."

Any effort to investigate the universe, whether through
science or literature, involves making a cut in the universe,
interrupting its wholeness and unity, and therefore dis-
rupting and ignoring the interconnectedness of all things.
Any investigation, whether poem or laboratory experiment,
involves saying "certain things are relevant to this investigation and certain things are not," and once this necessary cut

has been made, we have eliminated any possibility of seeing nature and the universe as a whole, in its entirety.

And from Bronowski later in the same book:

> The act of imagination is the opening of the system so that it shows new connections. I originally put this idea in *Science and Human Values* when I said that every act of imagination is the discovery of likenesses between two things which were thought unlike. And the example that I gave was Newton's thinking of the likeness between the thrown apple and the moon sailing majestically in the sky. A most improbable likeness, but one which turned out to be (if you will forgive the phrase) enormously fruitful. All acts of imagination are of that kind. They take the closed system, they inspect it, they manipulate it, and then they find something which had not been put into the system so far. They open the system up, they introduce new likenesses, whether it is Shakespeare saying, "My Mistres eyes are nothing like the Sunne" or it is Newton saying that the moon in essence is exactly like a thrown apple. All those who imagine take parts of the universe which have not been connected hitherto and enlarge the total connectivity of the universe by showing them to be connected.

The creative person, whether scientist or artist, according to Bronowski, is that person who imagines new, different connections, broadening our conception of the universe and its interconnectedness as a whole.

The complete creation of our cosmology then must definitely include the model given us by science, this constantly changing and growing model as science itself imagines and discovers new connections. We cannot turn aside from that.

But the scientific model must be further enhanced and infused by other human talents and genius making other new connections. The path to follow, it seems to me, is not contradicting or fighting or turning from science and its beautiful, invigorating story but assimilating it, incorporating its glory, celebrating both its findings and its method of scrutiny and openness, using its great power and stimulation and beauty as a jumping-off point to an energetic and meaningful spirituality. We are definitely and positively capable of finding and creating spirituality in this cosmology. We have the power and ability and possibly the obligation to do that. We must possess our cosmology rather than being possessed by it.

We can begin to do this by making those new imaginative connections as defined by Bronowski and also by examining imaginatively the questions we ask about nature and the universe.

In *Physics and Philosophy*, Werner Heisenberg states, "Natural science does not simply describe and explain nature; it is part of the interplay between nature and ourselves; it describes nature as exposed to our method of questioning."

C.S. Lewis echoes Heisenberg's thought in *The Discarded Image:* "Nature gives most of her evidence in answer to the questions we ask her."

What are the new and startling connections, the innovative questions we may ask of the sycamore leaf, of the wave against the beach, of the raven's call, of the play of a dandelion seed against the sky, of the hands of the lover, of our own involvement in the universe through our observation and delight in these phenomena? We must formulate new questions, ones that will definitely take into account and acknowledge those questions already asked. We must ask questions that accept and incorporate nature's revelations in response to the questions that science asks, but that utilize other realms of investigation, questions that make new connections, new metaphors.

If divinity should rise, not from the natural world alone, but from our interaction with the natural world, including our interactions with each other, if divinity is created through our manner of bestowing, our reverence, our praise and honor, the gifts we give, and if divinity comes into being likewise through our openness and willingness to receive, then we must ask the questions that allow and encourage these qualities to rise and manifest themselves.

And here's a miracle that must be constantly celebrated: in spite of those moments of the soul's desperation, we do proceed. We do proceed, even in the face of that "unyielding despair" that seems sometimes to be the result of the truths listed by Bertrand Russell. We do continue to attempt to build the soul's habitation. And we do it partially by expressing the awe and thrill and gratitude we feel at the mystery and beauty of the universe as it continues to reveal itself to us through all human disciplines. Being one ourselves with the universe, we continue to create it, to infuse it with meaning, as it continues to reveal and inform us, body and soul. We embrace strongly as we are in turn embraced by the stars, the heavens, the earth, embraced by the universe through our very revelry in it.

(1995)

( PART III )

# Rain

It rained all night last night, a slow rain. Its sound—thrumming on the roof, multiple tickings on each separate leaf of the poplar and maple near our bedroom—was very like a caress, gentle, steady. Before sleep, I watched it move in crowds of silver down the glass of the window. And later the rain entered my sleep. It was a cadenced voice delivering an important message in a foreign language I couldn't quite translate.

But once in my dreaming, I thought the voice was god's.

. . . . .

Rain is such a seemingly simple thing, so ordinary and commonplace. We all must have discovered it very early in our lives, earlier than we can remember. But how shocked we must have been at that first encounter. What an incredible phenomenon—water falling in pieces from the dark kneading and enfolding clouds of the heavens! How extraordinarily strange to move through air filled with water plummeting all around, the sun suddenly dimmed and even shadowed itself. As a friend once told me—watching his infant daughter encountering for the first time the details of our earth—with each new discovery her expression seemed to say, *And this too?!*

.     .     .     .     .

The world and everything in it becomes different in aspect in the rain. Rain elucidates and distinguishes with more precision than either sun or wind. It misses nothing, outlining the smallest crevices of iris, honeysuckle, sinking down into the funnels of trumpet vine and crawdad burrow, tracing each furrow in the bark of the oak, dripping off the lashes of green midge and moth, the feather barbs of mallard and coot. It lines the lines of every leaf and spear of marsh rushes, every pinpoint of the pine, calling attention to each spike of the burr, each gravel of the path. Nothing is overlooked, nothing too small for notice.

Rain even reveals new aspects of the self. Issa, an eighteenth-century Japanese poet, highlights this in one of his haiku:

> A sudden shower falls—
> and naked I am riding
> on a naked horse!
>
> (from *An Introduction to Haiku,*
> translated by Harold G. Henderson)

Drenched by the shower, wet as they both are, skin to skin, the man and the horse are altered, the sense of their bodies transformed by the rain.

. . . . .

And rain releases otherwise hidden fragrances—the sudden scent of wet cedar, of water-heavy seeded bluestem in an autumn field, puddle-filled oak leaves piled in ditches, the open earth damp and receptive. A hot cement sidewalk steaming with summer rain smells comforting, a fragrance of human neighborhood to me. The ethnobiologist Gary Nabhan explains the seemingly contradictory title of *The Desert Smells Like Rain* this way: "Once I asked a Papago youngster what the desert smelled like to him. He answered with little hesitation: 'The desert smells like rain.' The question had triggered a scent—creosote bushes after a storm, their aromatic oils released by the rains. The boy's nose remembered being out in the desert, overtaken: the desert smells like rain."

Rain not only unlocks the fragrances, it also enhances them. So says the poet Kyoshi:

> Clearing after showers,
> and for a little while the scent
> of hawthorn flowers . . .
>
> (from *An Introduction to Haiku*,
> translated by Harold G. Henderson)

And rain possesses fragrances solely its own, fresh sky-water in the wind, the cool, clean, sheet-snap fragrance of rain-coming, the trembling and rumbling slow-rising fragrance of rain-passing.

. . . .

I lived for a time once in an apartment on the twenty-third floor of a high-rise building. To my dismay, I found that I had no way of knowing for certain when it was raining unless I walked to the one window I had and looked down on the street. The rain passed invisibly and silently by my recessed window and me. I heard no sound of raindrops— the roof of the building was seven floors above me, the earth twenty-three floors below. There was little fragrance of rain falling through these city skies; it touched nothing as it flew by. I felt deprived, neglected, as if I'd been left out and ignored, not invited to the party.

. . . .

Watching rain raining on a lake or pond is mesmerizing. Few can turn quickly from the sight of raindrops striking in chaotic randomness every part of the surface of the water, then immediately losing themselves as they merge into the whole and disappear as separate entities. The resulting radiating rings cross and recross one another, circling, widening, each ring struck again and again by more rain, new rings constantly appearing and overlapping older ones. This vision is the vision we might see if we could see the pattern made by the pealing of many cathedral bells sounding over themselves and over the countryside. Nothing ever really ends or reconciles there. I think we recognize something mythic in that pattern, a basic truth of motion and structure and time, of becoming and dying, something about ourselves, about existence. Thus we are rapt, linked and bound to the watching.

. . . . .

Clean rain falling into the open mouth tastes like the essence of paradise. Rain tastes like life when kissed off the face of someone loved. I pity the stone heart of the moon for its lack of rain.

. . . . .

The last stanza of Robert Louis Stevenson's poem "Singing" suggests another transforming aspect of rain:

> The children sing in far Japan.
> The children sing in Spain.
> The organ with the organ man
> Is singing in the rain.

To sing in the rain is a different kind of singing, rather an act of effrontery, maybe even of defiant freedom, a most exuberant singing. Witness the famous song and dance of Gene Kelly in the movie *Singing in the Rain*. And to laugh with someone else in the rain is a laughter of exhilaration and abandon unlike any other. Some of us, like Samuel Beckett, feel we can even mourn a richer mourning in the rain:

I would like my love to die
and the rain to be falling on the graveyard
and on me walking the streets
mourning her who thought she loved me.

(#4 from *Quatre Poèmes*)

.     .     .     .     .

Rain is drama itself and the setting for drama. Hard rain in a thunderstorm is a true terror with its blue-white lightning rudely, angrily ripping the vista in half and the explosions of its thunder shaking the earth with long lingering rolls and growls. The thunderstorm in Shakespeare's *King Lear* is the perfect mirror for the inner torment and raging of the king.

In such a storm, all living things in the land seem to draw in, stop, motionless, attentive and wide-eyed, waiting, every cell alert, contemplative as Buddhas.

Thunderstorms demand our attention. And afterward, says Shiki:

The thunderstorm goes by;
on one tree evening sunlight—
a cicada cry.

(from *An Introduction to Haiku*,
translated by Harold G. Henderson)

We understand the meaning of peace.

.     .     .     .     .

Rain is generally considered a blessing and a beauty, a generosity. God "sendeth His rain on the just and on the unjust," says Matthew (5:45). When rain comes, it is a gift given indiscriminately—to the tumble bug and the beak of the June beetle, to the hairs of needlegrass and least weasel, the bristle of walrus and peccary, to the mouth of the rattle-snake, the mouth of the deer mouse, the pocket mouse, the thirsty elf owl, the skin of toad, the spines of the tarbush, alike to murderer, alike to saint.

Sings the psalmist, "Praise unto our God who covereth the heaven with clouds, who prepareth rain for the earth, who maketh grass to grow upon the mountains" (Psalm 147:8).

·  ·  ·  ·  ·

Rain is most often a gift nourishing the growing life of the earth. But I'm grateful too for all of its other facets and intricacies, its frights and its serenities, the foreign secrets and whisperings of its motion and coming, the person of its presence. It speaks, it gestures, it indicates, and I sense the universe, I sense myself, anew.

(1998)

# Born, Again and Again

I grew up near a small river in southwest Missouri, really a large creek, an easily navigable waterway with a calm current, deep in places, in others flowing with low white ruffles over rocky shoals. I went to this river often, as if to a favorite relative, to see what was happening, wading and swimming sometimes, watching the creatures of the bank shallows and shore sedges, a buzzard or two slowly spiraling the sky, finches and sparrows prattling in the mat of wild brambles. The fragrances of spring blackberry and sassafras, the spicy scent of summer grasses, the musty cold of damp, autumn leaves, hickories, walnuts, oaks rooting in the river's domain—I found them all.

One summer afternoon I went to this river with my parents and brother and another family. Together we were an ecclesia, as they called it, a word from the fundamentalist religion my parents had just joined. I went to the river this time for a baptism by immersion. Mine. I was thirteen. Words would be said. Transformations would take place, I was told. What would the river be then, I wondered, a participant in a religious ritual? Every religious ritual I had ever known had been performed inside a church sanctuary, out of the wind, away from the sunlight and the yes-commotion always present under an open sky, in a subdued church sanctuary enclosed by stained glass, lined with heavy wooden pews, the soldier-like brass pipes of an imposing organ standing at attention at one end, a choir in black robes, the minister in velvet. Baptism in my former church had meant a red rose dipped in water and held to an infant's head.

Beside the river on this day, they told me my sins would be washed away. I would be cleansed of all the sins of my thirteen years alive in Missouri and be born anew. I didn't doubt it, whatever my sins were. I already knew the river's chants and spells. I knew without knowing I knew that the river had something elemental to do with beat and blood, their risings and ceasings, everything to do with the trans-formations that happen when earth and sun and water come together, what emerges from that union breathing, grasp-ing, seeking and scrambling, suckling and nesting, what cacophony of webs, tones, carols, and spasms and spans sustain themselves within that union.

Inside the aura of ceremony, I walked into the river, meeting it as always, feeling the cool shore water on my feet, scattering a swirl of river-colored minnows, passing the black beads of a tadpole pod in the reeds, the circling of two water striders, down into the river's moving pres-ence, its flow stronger, colder, unrelenting, knocking a stick against my knee, wrapping a broken weed at my ankle. A knot of fishing line snagged on a small branch drifted by. I don't remember the words said as I balanced against the

current, but I went down over my head into the river's swath
and taste, its muffled silence, through the dim, broken light
of underwater sun, feeling the muddy leaves and slippery
stones of its base, a living fish bumping my shoulder, the
river sliding against my face, through my hair, far beneath
birds winging above faster than the current, down into the
force and time of the river's body.

And when I came up again and gasped the rash blaze
and explosion of summer, I believed wholeheartedly in river
belief. The river was here, tangible, soothing and biting,
cresting and waning, not a gift but an ongoing giving and
re-giving. The river, with all the being it spawned, was act-
ing. *River* was a verb not a noun. *Bank swallow, blue butterfly,
bumblebee, bittersweet* were not things but soaring and alight-
ing, bearing and consuming. *Wild grape* meant twining and
persisting, *dogwood* reaching, blossoming, seeding, withdraw-
ing, *perch* and *carp* and *catfish* pulsing, holding, enduring. The
river was being—swift, assertive, foresworn—moment by
moment by moment. And I knew I was joined in that same
being and supreme in the being of believing, moment by
moment by moment.

Later that afternoon we ate beside the river. We made
a small fire on the gravel bar, just large enough to recall
again the frenetic art of fiery vigor and brilliance, the art of
woodsmoke climb and fragrance. The river and our place
beside it took on the colors of evening. And the crickets
with their glass castanets, the frogs hidden near the water
with their long bass strums and trilling trebles, struck up
their defiant sounds of declaration, once the low melodic

call of an owl. The dim fire-points of the stars and the blinking fire-points of the lightning bugs in the heavy bank bushes transfigured the shore, the sky, the night. As the river grew darker, I could hear more distinctly the slow lap and easy slap of its moving waters. We gathered up then and started back, walking single file with flashlights along the narrow path.

I never regarded the river as a god. I would never have tangled it up in the vagaries of that word. Today, I remember, and I want to define *God* as unfolding, engendering, keeping, yielding. I want to imagine God, not static as the river is not static, as mountains are not static, as the stars are not static, as life is not static, but God as mighty empowering, urging, infusing, and coming and continual pressing against oblivion.

All the earth is engaged in this being. Every living entity—from the eelpout on the bottom of the Arctic Ocean to the bar-headed goose flying over Mt. Everest to the golden orb-weaving spider of the mangroves to the giant forest hog of the Congo to the bent and twisted bristlecone pine in the ice of the Rockies to the beds of fluffgrass on the barren Mojave—every living entity is testifying to this and agreeing with me.

(2008)

## "For Me Mothers and the Mothers of Mothers . . . "

Recently my husband and I were on a trip with my grown son and out for a walk together when I noticed that my son wasn't wearing a belt. I asked him what had happened to his belt, and he said he'd forgotten to pack one. He added, in a slightly exasperated tone, that no one would notice but me anyway, because no one else would scrutinize him as closely as I did. This made me laugh, because I realized that he knew that I looked at him in a way no one else did. And he was right.

Mothers and their children.

I have two adult sons, and I write now about the nature of the bond, as I understand it, that exists between mothers and their children. I remember, after the birth of my first son, being astonished that all human beings had come into existence in the way my son had come to be. I couldn't understand how something so stunningly miraculous, so breathtakingly wonderful and basically inexplicable as conception and birth, could at the same time be one of the most common and ordinary events on earth, happening all around us all the time.

What pathetically ignorant creatures we are. We believe we know something; yet no description of a determined, silvery sperm penetrating an ovum, no vocabulary detailing the quivering division of cells, no depiction of the helix of DNA, no step-by-step explanation of the development of embryo and fetus, lessened at all the total bewilderment I felt when holding my own baby in my arms. I couldn't begin to explain the fact that he was here, a very particular human being with a particular name, having real, exact little feet, both of them fitting in one of my hands, and his own tiny hands that could clasp my finger tightly, and possessing his own demands, his own pleasures.

"What hath God wrought!?" a friend of mine wrote to me after the birth of her first daughter.

My concern and identification with my sons began with the moment I knew I was pregnant. I was at once committed to eating the right foods, taking the proper vitamins, staying healthy. I mustn't do anything to endanger the life or well-being of this human being coming. This was a responsibility of greatest degree. The watchfulness, the care, the love that began in those moments has never wavered in its intensity.

Most mothers feel a measure of awe in regard to their children, a continuing wonder at the very fact of their existence. I have watched the faces of new mothers as they gaze at their babies, gazing in the same way I gazed at mine, memorizing every contour of the lovely face like no other. I know that I could identify my sons from photographs of their ears alone, or their lips, their hands, even now, men that they are.

Was it Douglas MacArthur's mother who brought a ladder to West Point so that she could climb up to the second-floor window to check on her cadet son, quarantined with the measles? I understand that totally. And in the movie *The Grapes of Wrath*, when Ma Joad sees her adult son Tom standing outside in the yard, the first time she's seen him in four years, she looks him up and down intently, wanting to be satisfied that his body is fine. She questions him to make certain his spirit is still whole. The look of concern and pride on her face, the wonder at his existence, resonate with me. I know exactly the feelings behind that look. And Jane Darwell, who won an Academy Award for her role as Ma Joad, must have known too, because she got the look of the mother exactly right.

When my sons reached adolescence and suddenly were taller than I was and had feet larger than their father's and voices that sounded like men, when they actually began to make very funny and witty and insightful remarks, I was amazed once more, especially after so many years of raucous silliness from them, mischief and wildness. I thought they were the most glorious, most clever beings that had ever existed. It still amazes me that all other men are so ordinary, while my sons are shockingly beautiful, stupendously brilliant, and glow like the sun.

No one can convince me otherwise.

I know, I know, this is what particularly drives daughters-in-law to despair, and now that I have a son newly married, I'm trying hard to suppress this mild form of insanity, trying not to stare at my son, not question him about how he's feeling, if he's been to the dentist recently, if he needs new socks—trying, in other words, to treat him, as much as possible, as if he were a typical guy with typical virtues and typical faults, even though I know that's an obvious lie.

The instinct a parent has to nurture and protect a child can never be entirely suppressed. I remember the exact sound and pitch of my young son's scream when he fell off our backyard swing years ago and broke his arm. Still, today, if I hear a sound that rings with that same pitch and timbre, my heart stops, and every part of my body goes numb, even before I can articulate why. And going with my sons when they each turned eighteen and were required to register for the Selective Service made my breath tight, my hands cold, sweaty. Both were of draft age during the time of the Gulf War. I was angry at everything then, angry at the government, angry at old men who send young ones to war to be killed or injured, to kill and injure others, angry at circumstances, afraid for my sons.

If mothers had ever been allowed to take the places of their sons in battle, we would have a history of wars fought by middle-aged women.

Isak Dinesen's story "Sorrow-acre" from her *Winter's Tales* is a beautiful, perceptive, and complex story of a mother who loses her life from exhaustion after mowing an entire field of rye, with a sickle, in one day, by herself. She does this on a wager, in order to free her son from imprisonment. By the end of the tale, the reader is uncertain as to whether the tyrant landholder who proposed the wager has been cruel or kind to the mother in allowing her to save her son.

"So might now, to the woman in the rye field, her ordeal be triumphant procession? For to die for the one you loved was an effort too sweet for words."

I remember thinking once that instead of being instructed to love our neighbors as ourselves we should have been instructed to love our neighbors as a mother loves her child, for that love is almost always unconditional, steadfast, fervent, full of willing sacrifice, forgiving all. These clichés are unpopular and considered sentimental and naïve by some people today; the woman devoted to her children is often portrayed in exaggerated and ridiculous ways and then satirized in our literature and dramas; but in my opinion, these qualities of a mother's love are present and true and very important to the health of human culture.

I don't mean to underestimate the strengths of a father's love or the great importance of the father's steady presence in a child's life. My husband has always been here as a reliable balance to my feelings. He provides a necessary perspective and is a source of security and calm, possessing a love for our children differently demonstrated, and perhaps differently directed, but no less than mine. "Is there a father among you who will offer his son a snake when he asks for a fish, or a scorpion when he asks for an egg?" asks Jesus in Luke's gospel (11:11).

A few years ago I visited Normandy Beach. The day was clam. I was standing on the cliffs looking out at the perfectly placid, blue sea, wide to the horizon, just a scarce line of mist and haze far in the distance. The beach below was clear and smooth. All was quiet except for the slow ruffle of the surf, a few leaves shuffling easily in a mild ocean wind.

The scene was expansive, full of benign possibilities and promises.

I turned to look toward the land behind me, and there, stretching as far as I could see over the April lawns and the hills beyond, were rows and rows and rows and rows of white crosses, hundreds of them, overwhelming in their numbers, all standing still and cold and mute, each one signifying the violent death of some young boy the same age as my sons and their friends.

I didn't know the name of a single boy buried there, and yet I was staggered by the horror, tears falling. Those boys had young, beautiful bodies like my sons. They too were strong and full of the same kind of daring and vulnerability and optimism. For a brief moment, I felt an inclusive love and a union with those boys who had died fifty years before, and with the grief of their mothers, and for all anonymous human beings caught in the webs of tragic circumstances, as we all are caught in the unchanging facts of death and history, in the strictures of cultural demands, trapped in our inability to understand clearly and thoroughly, in our drive for self-preservation. In that moment, I knew what it meant to be human.

Awakened to our common dilemmas and failures, our common strengths and beauties, I could have forgiven anyone for anything. That union I felt bodily with all human beings came to me because of my love and identification with the lives of my sons.

Should we call this state of motherhood a mild form of insanity?

I would rather call it the strongest natural human bond we know, and one that ultimately holds the culture together.

For most human beings learn first of love, if they ever learn of love, through their mothers. Those earliest sensations of caring—the motion and feel of the hands that bathe and bring food and drink to the mouth, and the arms that lift and carry, the body that rocks and holds gently, the music of the voice as it sings in the reassuring tones used with infants, tones, as recent research shows, that are universal to all human cultures—these sensations come predominantly and regularly through the mother and establish with the infant the ability to both give and receive love.

She brings to her child his first impressions of the world. She is the one who will assure him first of a world that welcomes him, that recognizes and nurtures him. She will indicate to him who he is and what place he has, provide him with ways by which he can define himself.

What happens to the child who cannot rely on his mother, or any steady mother figure, the child who is constantly anxious about her care, her love, her presence, her support? Despite lacking language, a young infant is continually forming self-image. How is he to perceive the world and himself in it? As he grows, what secure basis of love can he turn to in order to determine his actions? He is in freefall, with no tether, having no loving care that is certain in his small universe. Surely that child has a handicap of doubt, a void in his heart that weakens his ability to make generous determinations and to act with circumspection, a handicap he must work to overcome all of his life.

Both as individual and as a society, we depend on the strength of the bond of love between mother and child. It is at the holding core of any magnanimous, resolute society. The society that demeans or becomes indifferent to this bond, that ridicules or denigrates it, that encourages, in whatever subtle ways, a disregard of it, that applauds and glorifies an abandonment of it, that extols actions that are in conflict with it, necessarily undermines its own strength. If we ever totally lose faith in that most basic bond of love, our ability to act with confidence, with courage and compassion, will diminish and ultimately fail.

Seven years ago my mother-in-law was dying a slow death, blind and almost totally deaf. My husband, leaving on a business trip one evening, was at the hospital with her, telling her goodbye, how many days he would be gone, when he would see her next. She insisted on being helped out of her bed, which was no easy task, so that she could stand up to hug him. As he was going, she said to him sternly, "Don't take any chances."

The guardianship of the mother ceases only with death.

Now I have a daughter-in-law, and I am beginning a new role, one that I assume with eagerness. A remark from my new daughter, passed on to me by her mother, will remain a treasure in my heart. Early in their acquaintance, when first describing my son to her mother, my daughter-in-law named, among his attributes that she found attractive, the fact that he loved his mother.

How lucky I am to have this son, how fortunate to have been given such a daughter.

(1997)

# Death and the Garden

A few months ago I witnessed something on television that affected me profoundly. I was watching a documentary on work being done by archaeologists in the Takla Makan desert in central China. Bodies from a little-known and lost culture had been exhumed from very ancient graves, bodies remarkably preserved by that climate. Two of the bodies were of a young mother and her baby, close to a year old. The mother's body had been mutilated. The scientists surmised, from evidence found in the grave with her, that she had been a sacrifice. She and her baby were buried with the body of someone who was obviously a revered leader. The baby was wrapped in a finely patterned blanket, the colors still preserved. His head was uncovered, just in the way he must have been wrapped when taken from the arms of his mother so many years ago. His mouth was open, his cries halted with his death by suffocation. His first baby teeth were visible. There was terror on that small face. One of the scientists carefully pulled the blanket aside to reveal the baby's hands closed in tiny fists on his chest, closed in the way so common to infants, small curled hands my mother used to call rosebud hands. The scientists had detected traces of tears, the salt of tears on his cheeks. He had been buried alive with his dead mother. No one to help. No one to care.

This story, the implications of this story, were horrifying to me, as so many stories in the history of humankind are horrifying. It haunts me still, not simply from imagining the terror of that scene, but from being brought starkly face to face again with all of the questions it raises. What do those deaths mean, happening in a foreign culture so very long ago, the deaths of the young mother and her baby, very real, very individual? How can we ascertain a purpose to their deaths within any grand, overall scheme of things? And is there a grand scheme? If so, who is responsible for it, who is its architect, and who are we in this time and place within that scheme? What is our role? What are our responsibilities? How can we determine these things, being so ignorant, being so suffused in mystery?

I cannot bring myself to conclude that those deaths and the suffering preceding them happened for nothing. I cannot reconcile myself to the thought that they meant nothing. Dust to dust, ashes to ashes, vanished as the grass of the field, life as "a tale told by an idiot, full of sound and fury signifying nothing"—I cannot reconcile myself to that kind of oblivion for any living thing. The deaths of that mother and her baby were mighty and significant. I am certain they shook the web of being. I know the bonds connecting all living things trembled with the vacancy of those moments. Every death, whether creature or flower, whether a thousand pine needles of the forest or a weak hatchling pushed from its nest or a whale stranded on a beach or a deer starving on the plains, this mother and this child, each and every death is mighty and significant. There is a steady presence, a physical core of spine or heart, that will not allow me to turn that thought to its negative.

I believe every life and every death is of ultimate concern to a divinity, to a goodness, to the glory inherent to creation. Our species has put forward the tenet that a benevolence existing in the universe is aware of every faltering and final fall. "Are not two sparrows sold for a farthing? And one of them shall not fall on the ground without your Father" (Matthew 10:29). I hold to this tenet. Nothing dies in vain, nothing perishes unrecognized, nothing dies alone.

Perhaps every death on Earth has been in the nature of a sacrifice—the piled carcasses of bison, drowning wildebeests in migration, fledgling storks on the parched Serengeti, the hare in the jaws of the fox, the mouse in the talons of the hawk, the brother dying of tuberculosis, the sister of typhus, the soldier-son dead beneath the skies. Perhaps all deaths are necessary sacrifices to a final completion of the universe we cannot fully comprehend, death being an unavoidable part of this evolutionary process moving toward fruition.

We want to believe there is a pattern, a purposeful structure to the myriad of baffling events we witness in the physical world. We work to discern and create this structure. And we want to believe that life and death and our behavior within this structure, within the evolving universe, have significance. Maybe human behavior can influence the direction of the evolutionary process the universe ultimately takes. After all, our actions and our creations possess reality. Like atoms or spatial dust or ocean tides and currents or solar winds, our actions and our creations are threads in the warp and weft of physical phenomena. They too must determine the pattern, the story, the quality of the cloth being woven. Honesty and justice, compassion and courage, faith and forgiveness, praise and blessing brought into being by our behavior, introduced into the universe by our actions, must surely influence the essence, form, and beauty of the world's ultimate tapestry.

Here is a marvelous amazement: what appears with very clear evidence to be a chaos of stars and galaxies at various stages of existence in the heavens around us, what appears to be the random shifting of the continental plates on Earth, the seemingly senseless rising and falling of mountains and seas and the destruction attending those events, the massive extinctions of species, the disappearance of multitudes of civilizations and their peoples, somehow all of this evidence suggesting a universe indifferent to individual life, and our existence has hardly eliminated the powerful notion we have that the very opposite is true. Despite all this evidence, it seems impossible to rid ourselves entirely of the notion that there is purpose and meaning to what we witness and that we are an essential and unique part of the web of being. We live with this notion. We base decisions on it. We act with honor and sacrifice depending on it.

Perhaps we should trust this notion implicitly, embrace it, hold to it as certainly as we hold to the confidence of morning coming, to the inevitability of evening passing. For this notion of ours is obviously earth-bred. It has risen with us out of the earth just the same as the giant redwoods, the river sedges, and the tundra lichens have risen, just as flocks of snow geese or a newly emerging damselfly, just as the sockeye and the coho rise. All of these rise without question, without doubt, in full faith, adhering to the intentions of their beings. The belief that neither in life nor in death is any entity forgotten and that our conduct has significance, this belief is part of the definition of our being too, part of the fact and fulfillment of our being. It is a belief made of the earth; for we are made of the earth. It is a belief that is inherent to us. We possess it as we possess our hands and our eyes and our words. It occupies a signal place in our name and in the final meaning of our name.

With this belief comes the conviction that we have obligations to fulfill. The same silent stars in their grand array of shining hydrogen and helium refer to this. The moon is eloquent on equal justice. The wind passing through rocky arroyos and icy gorges is precise on determination. The shadows of winter willows stirred by wind describe grace and serenity. Even in its fleeting gestures, the river holds with certainty the noonday light. We recognize these languages. They reaffirm our sense of obligation. They echo our intuitions. They resound through the most fundamental origins of our art and music and literature. We repeat them in our prayers. We turn to them in our love songs.

Our species, in all ages and in all cultures, has longed for a vanished garden, a holy garden, pure and blessed, absent of suffering, terror, destruction, and violence, a garden no living human has ever experienced and yet a garden that seems to us to have substance. But every time we believe we might step into such a garden, it disappears. Maybe that garden, that state of fully realized justice and beauty, is a potential destiny toward which the universe is tending. Maybe we actually carry this future garden in the central blood marrow of our bones, in our most ancient and deeply protected genes. And so it is we remember this garden though we have never known it, possess this garden while continually longing for it, hold it close though forever seeking it. I believe all those who have lived before us have died in some measure for the sake of this garden and in the hope of its coming. I believe a benevolent and longing power trusts us and depends upon us to work with all our strength and faith to deliver this vision into reality, to carry this promised home into its home.

(1999)

# Cradle

I cannot think of anything more important for the future of the earth than that we have loving, diligent mothers and fathers caring for our children. Nothing. We can write books and make speeches and conduct research and discuss data and theories and hold seminars and establish educational programs and pass laws and levy fines and set aside wilderness areas and protect endangered species, but none of these will make much difference to the future well-being of the earth unless we have children entering adulthood who are confident enough of their own worth to be able to love generously, to give to others, to make sacrifices, to restrain their desire for possessions—adults who understand how honesty, loyalty, justice, and benevolence come into being only through personal action.

If children learn to act with compassion by being treated compassionately themselves, if they learn to love by being loved, to respect others by having received respect, to cooperate by being involved in cooperation, to keep their word by experiencing honesty, to protect others by having been protected themselves—how can we possibly overestimate the importance of children being nurtured by dependable parents who are capable of demonstrating such qualities? It will be these qualities that will form the basis for all future decisions our children must make regarding their interactions with other people and the natural world.

For these reasons, the reliable presence of the attentive mother in a child's life has always seemed crucial to me. No one loves a child with a forgiving and enduring love like his or her own mother. No one else is so intensely concerned with her children's welfare, no one else so fierce in the defense of her child, no one else so quick to allay fears, to reassure, no one else so attentive to her child's needs. In those early years of life when a child is unsure and awkward, lacking skill with language, attempting to negotiate in a world of often critical and commanding adults without fully understanding what is expected, there must be a shelter, a place of steady love and acceptance. That place of trust is most often the mother.

Before the births of my own children, when I was teaching school, I used to watch my kindergarten children waiting for their mothers to come for them at the end of the day. I always saw an intense joy and confidence on the face of each one as his or her mother came into sight: "This is *my* mother." That same joy was never quite there for any other adult.

The security and love given by a father is very important also, of course. I loved my own father dearly, and I remember the feeling I had as a young daughter when held in his arms. (A friend once told me that as a child in bed alone in the dark at night he always felt the world was safe as long as he could hear his father's voice.) I'm certain my confidence in my father's love has contributed to my feelings of confidence in the existence of a protective, benevolent divinity, a cognizant and responsive universe in which I possess value and purpose. And, as a mother, I could explain things to my sons, but they needed their father at every stage of their growth in order to come to some understanding of what a man is. But for now my emphasis is on the role of the mother, and, to paraphrase Adrienne Rich: Every child deserves a mother who thinks he, or she, is a miracle.

Being a mother is a hard job to do well. It's a job that demands time and concentration—it can't be hurried, it can't be scheduled. It requires intelligence, creativity, patience, and stamina. It involves emotional risk, an identification with the body and soul of another human being, a giving that is unique. The work of love is exquisitely painful, my friend Jim Whitehead once said to me long ago.

Almost any other employment or profession can seem to offer a brighter future, less emotional risk, more tangible rewards (a paycheck), respect given more often by the community. (I wouldn't want to count the times I've heard the question, "Do you work or are you a housewife?") No wonder so many women, despite bearing children, have largely abandoned the responsibilities of being mothers, to the detriment of the society and its ability to act with prudence and circumspection.

Many women, in circumstances beyond their control, must work outside the home, and children of these mothers need special attention from friends and relatives. If one of the reasons for marriage is to establish an environment for raising healthy children, then keeping the family unit intact will allow many mothers the option of being at home with their children, at least through those very early years when self-image and important attitudes toward life are being formed.

I was recently reminding one of my sons, who is grown now, of an incident in his childhood when he was around eight years old. My father had passed away that year. Before his death he'd given my son a BB pistol that shot a single BB, loaded one at a time. My son came rushing into the house one day after school shouting that he was going to get his BB pistol and shoot Timmy Gilmore, an infamous neighborhood bully.

I followed him in his fury into his bedroom attempting to find out how he'd been hurt, what had happened, trying to urge him to consider other courses of action, hoping not to be forced to embarrass him by restraining him physically.

"Grandpa would want me to do this," he shouted in anger, evidencing an impression of manhood—protecting the dignity of the family—that had somehow been conveyed to him. This stance hurt me in its pathos—a young boy attempting to live up to the conceived image of his grandfather who was gone.

Well, my son didn't shoot anybody with his BB pistol, that day or any other. I listened and sympathized with his outrage until his temper cooled and we could talk a little more about his pistol and about people who do cruel things.

We were laughing about this affair, because my adult

son, a thoughtful, levelheaded individual, is so different from this angry child bent on physical violence, when my other son, who was reminiscing with us, said to me, "But what if you hadn't been there?"

Children need our attentive presence. Despite their many virtues, children are not born civilized, and I mean by that not born knowing how to negotiate the world with self-control, courtesy, and restraint. Most mothers, when they turn their full attention to their children, are so good at helping them acquire these qualities, so very good at being mothers. They can easily become experts at it—feeding, nursing, comforting and encouraging, dressing and bathing (not simply as chore but as communication with careful hands that cherish and respect), listening, correcting and sympathizing, teaching the stories and songs, teaching the language, daily defining for the child what being human can and must mean.

There is a difference between maintaining children and nurturing children, the difference between feeding the body and feeding the soul. How do we best nurture children? I think we begin by all of us, the whole society, everyone, acknowledging the skill and love and time it takes to do the work properly, emphasizing again and again and never forgetting how important it is that the job be done well, both for the society of human beings and for the health of the natural world. We must recognize and encourage, with all moral and practical support possible, those that are engaged in the task.

I say without hesitation that nothing done on this earth

is more important *for* the earth than what mothers and fathers together have the power and talent to do.

. . . . .

Children are highly intelligent, capable creatures who have a unique rapport with the natural world. I often prefer their company to the company of adults, simply for their wide-ranging curiosity, their ease and delight with the earth, their openness and flexibility.

Anyone who has been around children and paid attention to them is aware of these qualities. I remember noticing my two-year-old son one cold autumn morning hunkered down on the sidewalk looking closely at a small gathering of water. When I got down on the sidewalk and looked too, I saw tiny needles of ice, white and crystalline, perfectly aligned, circling the pool of water. Understanding his wonder at seeing such strange and intricate beauty for the first time, I was captivated myself: Why and what was this beauty, this joy in the beholding?

And I agreed with my four-year-old son John, watching a small catfish he'd caught as it swam in its bucket of water, when he said to me in hushed and heartfelt tones, "It's the most beautiful thing I ever saw in my life."

"I brought my child into this world," I heard a young mother say. "The least I can do is let him show it to me."

Even adolescents can demonstrate an enlivening connection with the earth. Once when we were driving through the Front Range of the Rockies and had stopped at a scenic overlook, an old truck with three scraggly looking teenage boys came roaring in beside us. All three jumped out in their raucous, careless way, leaving the doors wide open, music blaring. One boy, bounding to the top of a boulder, looked out over the enormous valley below, the overwhelming blue rock mass of Mt. Evans rising in the background, and shouted in truly awestruck tones, "Holy Freak Show!"

My rather calm contemplation of the scene was suddenly charged with new exuberance.

Most children have a relationship with the earth we can learn from, a relationship of curiosity and acceptance, free of barriers or judgments, a melding of the body with the natural world. Adults, by acknowledging the intelligence and perception of children, by allowing themselves, when circumstances arise, to be taught by children (not in a patronizing way but with genuine attention and interest), are teaching that learning and curiosity are on-going activities, that questioning is an enjoyable pursuit, that it is not shameful to admit ignorance, that praise of all forms of life engenders strength. Listening carefully to children and considering what they have to say also gives them a measure of self-respect and enables them to obey adults more readily, without feeling constantly humiliated or demeaned.

One spring morning when we were living in Texas, I saw my son Artie, around two and a half at the time, follow our cat Moby into our garage. Dangling lifelessly from Moby's mouth was a small lizard, an anole, head hanging from the jaws on one side, thread of a tail swinging from the other.

Artie emerged from the garage a minute later carrying

the anole draped motionless as limp ribbon over his finger. Rather than the normal vivid yellow-green, the anole was an ashen, purple-gray. His eyes were lidded and sunken away. His tiny feet and hair-thin toes were drooping and still.

"He's dead, Artie," I said.

"He *not* dead," Artie said, emphatically.

"The cat caught him and killed him, Artie. He's dead," I repeated, pointing out the still eyes, the small tear in the skin at the anole's neck, the way the anole was lying stomach-up now, inert, unresponsive, head tilted back, in Artie's palm.

"He *not* dead," Artie insisted. "He not dead." There was something of faith in his tone.

So, to placate Artie, I got a paper cup, and we put the anole, who slid with no resistance at all, into the bottom of it. No need for a lid—he was dead. I put the cup on a windowsill in the kitchen and went on doing other things and so did Artie.

A few minutes later, working at the kitchen sink, I glanced at the cup, and behold! it was empty. For a moment, I had a surge of astonishment and joy that must have been at least a little similar to Mary Magdalene's when she saw the empty tomb with the stone rolled away.

And there, rushing up the bright window pane, was the "dead" anole, his body full and alert, pulsing sun-green, his agile legs and toes spread, his head cocked, his black eyes, deep as day, staring right at me.

Resurrection.

I had been wrong, not realizing how superbly anoles can

"play dead" as a defense mechanism. It gave me added joy to be able to say to Artie, "You were right! I was wrong. He's not dead."

Sometimes mothers know, and sometimes fathers know, and sometimes children know, and sometimes none of us knows, and that's the way life is, and we proceed together.

.    .    .    .    .

As unsettling or as comforting as it may be, it seems the most enduring lessons conveyed to children come not through language but through gesture and example. The motion and stance of the body rarely lie. They almost always reveal the soul. Children are quick to detect hypocrisy and to resent it. They are just as quick to detect its opposite and are inclined to cooperate with that honesty.

I was in a fast-food restaurant recently, sitting near a family—mother, father, two sons around six and eight, and a baby girl. The father got up carrying the trays of trash. The two boys went scrambling, running, and pushing after him. One boy stumbled, the other boy tripped over him and fell into the dad. A sundae cup dropped off the tray, splattering melted ice cream all over the floor. The boys, sprawled on the floor, were laughing, wild little darlings. The mother and dad looked resigned, like, "This is our life."

The dad and the two boys left and came back a moment later with napkins, and all three of them, the dad too, got down on the floor together and wiped up the ice cream. The boys were not scolded, not humiliated. There were no long lectures, yet the lesson was very clear: Men take responsibility for the consequences of their actions. Bless that dad.

This isn't a new thought—that actions speak louder than words—but it seems especially true in regard to children. Those intuitions and feelings of reverence that we call spiritual are communicated most genuinely to children through example.

My husband is fond of recalling an incident that occurred when he was young, a Boy Scout in Missouri. He was camping with his troop at Camp Osceola near the Osage River one summer night, inside his sleeping bag inside his tent. He remembers being awakened deep into the night by his scoutmaster. He and the other boys were told to get up, not to talk, that they were all going somewhere. The scoutmaster then led them through the forest of hardwoods, among the black trees steady with the stillness of night, up to a rock promontory high above the river and its valley.

It was clear and moonless. There were no trees on the rock bluff, and the entire night sky, completely filled with stars, was visible above them. The boys lay down on the earth and watched the sky in silence. No one said anything.

After a while, the scoutmaster said it was time to go and led the boys back to their camp.

Recalling that night, my husband says that when he was previously inside his tent and in his sleeping bag, he felt he was defined, that he knew where he was and who he was. But when suddenly out beneath the night sky with its wide, descending history and moment of stars, he realized that he was part of something very much larger than his family, his troop, or this piece of ground in Missouri. He was part of the universe, part of something magnificent and beautiful and grand in its mystery.

Surely that scoutmaster had faith both in the power of the universe to reveal itself and in the power and sensitivity of a boy to receive that revelation, and his faith was demonstrated in his action, communicated through the sacredness of his silence.

Divinity in the scoutmaster's action, divinity in the stars in the sky in the night, in human perception, divinity in the faith in divinity.

May all parents possess similar faith.

Something good happens to the body and to perception when gratitude is expressed for the life we experience, not for life in general, but thanks for the particular form of life in the particular moment, because that is the most genuine and vibrant kind of thanks—for the gold of a low sun off the columbine by the fence, for the endurance of this old, tangled apple tree with only one branch still living, for this child in my lap in this big chair by the window, for the bounding river, which is and is not, before me this very evening, which is and is not.

Gratitude expressed for the life of the moment bestows honor. Honor thus bestowed takes on the form and power of that specific life and returns to the giver the ability to forgive, to experience the expansive vision from which forgiveness of ourselves and others proceeds.

It is difficult to harbor hatred while walking at night across a snow-covered field blue with the moon and its shadows, to remain resentful surrounded by rocking summer grasses and coneflowers, a scatter of boulders rich with lichen. Jealousy and spite appear weak and ridiculous when seen against a sweeping world of currents and sky reflections, skating water striders, darters, minnows, the easy motion of mosses in the branching rootstocks beneath a pond lily.

We are not perfect people and neither are our children. But nature provides all the space and perspective we need to accept error, to create forgiveness. Honor and praise for our life, offered in whatever manner seems most efficacious—whether through literature or song, math or visual arts, dance, the sciences, or simply through contemplation or an insightful question—is a form of prayer. During moments of such prayer, we might be able to move with a grace beyond ourselves. We must believe that our children will recognize this motion when it occurs and seek to emulate it in their own lives.

We can provide our children with opportunities to witness this prayer: in friends who love the earth, in musicians, artists, and writers who express our aspirations and our dilemmas, "the human heart in conflict with itself," in clowns and comedians who reveal our foolishness and pomposities, in scholars, scientists, and craftsmen whose passion and dedication to their work is evident, in other mothers and fathers and grandparents who give time and love to their children.

Some gestures of prayer may seem slight and transient at the time. Once on a cold March morning when I was a child, my mother called my brother and me excitedly to the window to see something in our backyard. I remember being disappointed that it was only a new cluster of purple crocus in bloom against the dead grasses. This whole incident took only a moment, and I am certain I must have uttered some remark like, "Is that all?" And yet my memory of this moment is vivid—my mother's delight, the reassurance in those brave first flowers of spring.

When our sons and daughters are grown, they might occasionally recall something of what we said to them during their childhoods, but it's certain they will always remember in their bodies how we lived, how we moved through time, the music and rhythms of our interactions within the family, within the society, within the natural world, what we valued, what we celebrated, how we encountered tragedy, how we defined failure and success. As adults, these memories will be as integral to them as breath and pulse.

·   ·   ·   ·   ·

> Flesh of flesh
> Bone of my bone thou art and from
> thy state
> Mine never shall be parted,
> weal or woe.
>
> *John Milton, "The Eternal Bond"*

Without self-respect, it is difficult for any child or adult to understand how to respect the earth and other living beings. Without a sense of personal integrity, it is difficult for any child or adult to honor the integrity of the earth and those that live here with us. Without being loved with a love so steady and complete that its presence goes unnoticed, it is difficult for a child to know that such a love is possible or how to give a similar love to other human beings and to the life of the earth.

All people in all times have faced obstacles in their efforts to fulfill their obligations, to maintain their dignity and compassion, to live moral lives. Some have encountered more severe adversities than others—those touched by wars and famines, extreme poverty, incurable diseases and epidemics, oppressive governments, disintegrating social structures. Within their particular circumstances all individuals have had to make difficult decisions in their attempts to live good and giving lives, often having to act counter to the popular notions of the time.

We are no different. We face our own challenges, those peculiar to our times and our individual circumstances. Today social and economic forces have put strains on the family and on many bonds that hold our communities together, and children have suffered as a result. I have seen them suffer myself—young children in schools where I have taught, children I have cared for, friends of my sons.

Children don't need an abundance of goods. They never have. They do need and deserve the enduring solicitude of both of their parents together, whenever at all possible, mother and father maintaining the family and sharing their children's history from birth through adulthood.

It hasn't been the fashion in recent years to keep promises, whether those promises were made publicly as in marriage vows, or whether those promises were implicit as those made to a baby conceived and brought into the world or to the earth upon which we depend. If we break faith with others, especially with our babies who are the embodiment of faith, what is to keep us from breaking faith with the earth as well?

If we will not take time from individual interests to be with our children and to create stable, loving homes where they can thrive, it seems unlikely that either we or our children will ever take the time or make the sacrifices necessary to ensure the health and well-being of the earth, the first cradle and nurturing home of us all.

As we work to understand the concerns of raising children, how to proceed, desiring always the best future for the children we love and the earth we so revere, we know we can turn for strength to those things in the universe that we trust and from which we take comfort—perhaps the affirmation of life in the cellophane wings of a neon-blue dragonfly hovering mid-air, or the feel of someone loved close by in sleep, maybe the call of a cardinal and the subsequent discovery of his bright scarlet high in a winter oak, or the churning, boiling fright of the hot sun in the sky at noon, or the assertion in a gene of pollen flying from a blossom of wild strawberry—that elusive divinity as it comes to us and recedes from us in its myriad and glorious manifestations.

(1995)

# A Covenant with Divinity

It was a summer day. I was five or six years old, no older. I was running fast down a sidewalk in our neighborhood, heading for home, when I stumbled and fell, my bare knees skidding on the cement. Sitting on the sidewalk, crying and holding my bleeding knees, I remember uttering in bewilderment and anger, "Why did God make me fall? Why did He make me fall?" This is a startlingly clear memory of mine, a signal moment that stands out in my recollection of past experiences. If you and I were in that neighborhood now, I could show you the exact spot where I fell.

What was the concept of God I had at this young age that initiated such a question? Where had that concept come from? Without then knowing the words "omniscient" or "omnipotent" or "predestination," the message I had received from the religious teachers around me, from hymns and songs and certain Bible stories, from hearing comments made by adults during times of death and tragedy, was that God was a hugely powerful, perfect creature, both fearsome and loving, who had created everything in the world, was present everywhere, aware of everything and controlling everything, all past history and future events, and who operated with purposes often mysterious to human beings. I couldn't have said this in those words at five or six years old, but this was the concept I had incorporated into my attempts to understand the way the world operated.

That question, "Why did God make me fall?" has at its heart issues many of us are still struggling with. Where is God in our sufferings and in the sufferings of others? I come back to the issue again and again. Why should pain, suffering, evil, and violent destruction exist in a world created by an all-powerful, all-knowing, all good and perfect God? How is this seeming contradiction to be resolved?

It is important to me to possess a vision of divinity that does not contradict our reason or our understanding of the universe today. While that vision will always require faith and an openness to the spiritual, it will only be weakened if it conflicts with our contemporary understanding of the physical world, an understanding that influences the way we define ourselves and upon which we base many decisions in our daily lives. Most definitions of *god* in cultures in the past have been in union with their cosmologies. Our cosmology, our story of the physical universe, tells us that the Earth in its long history has passed through many stages—large ice fields advancing from the poles and retreating, ocean levels rising and falling. From the fossil record we can trace the appearance and the extinction of thousands of species. We know that the continental land masses drift on tectonic plates and that mountains form from pressures on the land when these tectonic plates meet. We have geologic evidence of catastrophic events that occurred on Earth before the existence of humans, collisions with meteors and asteroids that caused massive explosions resulting in drastic changes in the earth's atmosphere. We can locate the craters left by these collisions. Not long ago, I stood in Arizona on the high, dusty rim of such a crater, the result of a meteor striking Earth fifty thousand years ago with the explosive force of twenty million tons of TNT. People standing on the opposite rim of this shockingly deep and gaping depression in the land looked very small. Today we realize that we are immersed in a vast array of cosmic events and that at this moment stars in the heavens are being born and stars are dying. All the physical phenomena we witness are in flux and change.

Where is a god in this physical universe of constant changes, changes that often cause suffering and the deaths of humans and other life on Earth? Where is a good god in the destruction caused by earthquakes, hurricanes, tornadoes, volcanic eruptions? Where was this good, powerful god in the sufferings of the many, many children who died in the past from diseases like cholera, typhoid, tuberculosis, smallpox, malaria, polio, scarlet fever?

I went with my mother once to visit a very young girl dying of leukemia. She looked small and vulnerable lying in a large bed set up for her in the living room of her home. I thought she was beautiful. And as I remember it now, everything around her was white except for a gray kitten playing on the bed beside her. Her mother had a quiet, cordial manner. She was wearing a plain house dress of the type worn by women in the 1940s. She was an ordinary woman, except for the expression of pain on her face, the deep grief in her eyes.

The attempt to justify suffering, of the innocent especially, generally requires accepting either the conclusion that the human species deserves to suffer or that the ways of an omnipotent God are simply a mystery to mankind and it is a matter of faith to believe that suffering results in some good, if we could only understand it. Neither conclusion is satisfying to me. Each implies that an all-powerful, all-good God is either causing or allowing the suffering of innocents to occur. If medical science had accepted either of these conclusions, none of the discoveries of modern medicine that have saved lives and relieved suffering would have taken place.

I believe in a creative power that is the source of all beauty and energy and goodness in the universe. I believe this power is divine and benevolent and longs for us and needs us. Rare and unpredictable moments come occasionally that convince me of this. A few evenings ago I was standing outside alone, surrounded by a warm, easy wind in the autumn trees, the constant insistence of crickets, the call of a night bird. A dog was barking far away. Even the light of the moon seemed to me a significant sound. And in that moment, I was certain that a benevolent presence in the universe lingers expectantly, yearning for us as a mother might yearn for her child's first word, as a mother might yearn for her daughter's life.

I believe the divine power and the universe both are in

the process of coming fully into being. The physical universe is in constant change. Its creation is not finished. It is still roiling and trembling, shuddering and exploding, alive with slow and steady change. Suffering and death are often the results of this necessary ongoing creative process. And we are not complete. Divinity, as manifested in the universe, is not complete. It also is in the process of moving toward its magnificent and fully realized existence. By our actions and our faith, we may play a role in the direction the evolution of the universe and the power within it take.

We have witnessed, in the rise of living forms on Earth, a co-creation occurring over time. This is particularly evident in the development of flowering plants and their pollinators, each needing the other for survival, influencing the physical form of each other, both rising together simultaneously. Consider how perfectly bees and the wildflowers of their regions require and serve each other. They didn't accidentally find each other one day. Each has survived by modifying and determining the form and life habits of the other.

Co-creation is also evident in the development of the human thumb and the brain. The more the thumb was used by early humans, the larger the portion of the brain became devoted to its manipulation, thus the more adept the thumb became and the more it was used and so on. The hands and the brain influencing each other gradually became capable of molding a cup, bandaging a wound, threading a needle, building an arch, grinding the lens of a telescope, fashioning a violin, drawing the bow, fingers on the strings, engaging the heart.

Maybe co-creation is the way it is with humans and divinity, each shaping and influencing the strength and presence of the other, an ongoing co-creation. The Bible speaks often of a covenant between God and people. A covenant involves promises made between two parties, each needing the other, each agreeing to fulfill certain obligations to the benefit of the other. I believe the power of divinity is enhanced, becomes actualized, as we recognize its presence and express its being. We, in turn, are altered, filled with energy and strength and beneficence during the process of that recognition.

Believing that the divine power and human beings act as co-creators pleases me, because it does not separate the divine from the ways of the physical universe as we understand them today, and because it does not lead to blaming an all-powerful god for suffering on the earth or to the futile question of why an omnipotent god should "allow" or "cause" the suffering of innocents. It does not present a god as a master puppeteer controlling all the strings of the universe. It enables me to be in sympathy with the creative power, to feel that what I do and say may matter to the future development of the universe and the fulfillment of divinity.

In the poem "The Possible Suffering of a God during Creation," I express compassion for the divinity, suggesting this god too feels grief for the suffering "that the duration / of the creation must, of necessity, demand . . . "

. . . How can he tolerate knowing
There is nothing else here on earth as bright and salty
As blood spilled in the open?

Maybe he wakes periodically at night,
Wiping away the tears he doesn't know
He has cried in his sleep, not having had time yet to tell
Himself precisely how it is he must mourn, not having had
    time yet
To elicit from his creation its invention
Of his own solace.

We may be the means by which the universe comes to love and console itself. These thoughts imply obligations undertaken willingly and gladly, because we understand that we are living in a world that is not finished. As suffering and death and evil are the results of this necessary ongoing creative process, so also are life and all that sustains us—summer swimming in slow, grandfather rivers, early-morning grasses fiery with frost, rakes and hoes, gardens and garden gates, workers on the roof singing in the hot sun (I heard them this afternoon), slapstick, *Im wunderschönen Monat Mai*, all moments of serenity, all moments of bliss.

We comfort each other during times of suffering and grief, uncertainty and fear. All of us in this country have experienced these emotions very recently. When humans commit violent acts against one another, the divine presence in the universe suffers. Divinity is wounded. Perhaps it is necessary in times like these to comfort this divine power also by expressing our continuing faith, by praising life, by struggling to deal with complicated and dangerous situations in the best ways we can understand, by helping and loving each other and the world. God too so loves the world. We work to fulfill the obligations placed on us as creatures aware of ourselves and aware of the existence of the physical world and the divinity within that world. We know we are working together with the divine power. It is leading as we are leading. It is the source of compassion and forgiveness as we are the agents of compassion and forgiveness. We are infused with divinity ourselves, multiplying the place and power of divinity, as we discover, express, and extol its presence in the universe.

(2001)

# Surprised by the Sacred

Driving on a paved road not far from home last summer, I saw an injured snake, hit by a car, stuck by its open wound to the road. It was curling and writhing, struggling to free itself. I stopped and went back, thinking to move it from the hot, bare road and into the shade and shelter of the weeded ditch where I felt it would eventually die, yet possibly suffer a little less.

As I reached the snake, lying on its back, twisted around its wound, and bent to move it, it took one very sharp, deep breath, a gasp so deep I could see its rib cage rise beneath the ivory scales along its upper body, and, in that moment, it died. It lay suddenly without moving, not at all the existence it had been, inexorably altered in being. And its gasp and the dying were simultaneous, the breath stopped, held within the narrow width of its dead body forever.

I was stunned in that moment by an awareness of order and union: the snake at my fingertips had been a living creature, drawing breath as I draw breath, taking air into its body. *Living*—the word was suddenly expanded for me in meaning, in impact. It now embodied a compassion of connection wider, more powerful, and more undeniable than any I had perceived before.

One definition of *sacred* is to be declared holy. I would declare this moment to be a sacred moment in my life, and I would declare the elements composing this moment—the struggling snake, its life ceasing, the vision of its breathing, the unrelenting summer sun, the steady buzz and burr of the insects in the weeds around us, the fragrance of dry grasses, the boundless blue of the heavens—holy in their bearing of essence and divinity.

A similar moment of enlightenment, also involving a snake, is recounted in D. H. Lawrence's poem "Snake." On a hot summer day, the speaker of the poem comes upon a snake drinking at his water-trough.

> He sipped with his straight mouth,
> Softly drank through his straight gums, into his slack long
>     body,
> Silently . . .
>
> He lifted his head from his drinking, as cattle do . . .
> And flickered his two-forked tongue and mused a moment,
> And stooped and drank a little more.

As the speaker watches, he thinks he should kill the snake.

> But must I confess how I liked him,
> How glad I was he had come like a guest in quiet, to drink
>     at my water-trough
> And depart peaceful, pacified, and thankless,
> Into the burning bowels of this earth.

The underlying unity of life is revealed in that moment. All life—beautiful or reprehensible, dangerous or benign—

takes sustenance from the earth, all lips that drink, all throats and bodies and roots that seek water.

And all forms of life are one in their tenacity, in their determined grip on existence, in their unfaltering will to be, exhibited so obviously in the sow thistle rising through any crevice forced or found in cement or rock; in mayweed and burdock thriving along roadsides, among rubbish and waste; in the unrelenting persistence of birds—sparrows, crows, warblers—up at dawn, even after a sudden spring storm of sleet and ice, a long frigid night, calling and scrabbling in the cold, there to survive, crisis or no. "Urge and urge and urge / Always the procreate urge of the world," Walt Whitman wrote.

This kinship of being, of devotion to life, once recognized, demands respect for each living entity in its place. Another definition of *sacred* is venerable, worthy of respect.

My family moved to a farm in Missouri when I was fifteen. Along with the purchase of the farm, we inherited a herd of sheep, just at lambing season. It was a painfully cold, late January, and when twins were born, it was often necessary to bring one lamb into the house to keep it from freezing while the ewe took care of the other. Even today, many years later, I can see those newborn lambs, whiter and cleaner than the snow they lay on at birth, each so immediately out of the warm, wet womb into the wide winter cold, the unfathomably deep, gray skies, the world wholly new to their eyes just opened, and, hanging from each lamb, the drying string of a bloody umbilical cord.

I've never felt anything again so soft as the fleecy silk of those young lambs, silk so soft it was barely discernible against my fingertips, the sensation enhanced by the feel of the thin, warm body beating beneath. I remember having one of my fingers accidentally mistaken for a nipple and taken quickly into a lamb's mouth, the surprisingly strong sucking and gripping power of that tongue and throat on my finger. Life is this important, this crucial.

We seem to be creatures who need physical sensation, tangible objects to imbue with the abstractions that mean so much to us as a species—innocence, compassion, peace. Each of the newborn lambs we cared for during those years of my adolescence has come to be for me the very feel, the sound, the living body of faith, of purity, and of hope. These are the same virtues many people in the past believed were presented to God in the sacrifice of unblemished lambs. "Behold the Lamb of God," John the Baptist announces when he sees Christ walking toward him out of the crowd.

The newborn lambs of my adolescence entered the world bearing this history in their being, in their bodies—stories of the sacred. And they were dear to me, their presence enhanced, because of the stories they bore.

The surprise of encountering unusual juxtapositions can also bring awareness of the amazingly divine carnival of life, this sacred circus that surrounds us—the juxtaposition of a tomcat sleeping with a fallen forsythia blossom on his head, a toad found in the toe of a rubber boot, the disappearing and ephemeral form of ocean surf raging against implacable rock, the wild abandon and indifference of nature seen against the static of the man-made, as these lines from the Japanese poet Issa illustrate:

Out from the hollow
of Great Buddha's nose—
comes a swallow.

(from *An Introduction to Haiku,*
translated by Harold G. Henderson)

Once, in a muddy, ill-smelling chicken yard noisy with
cackling hens, I held in my hand one-half of a fertilized
chicken egg accidentally broken. In the center of that half
shell filled with golden yolk, a small dot of bright blood
pulsed regularly and steadily into a threaded network of
spreading red webs so small and fine they were hardly visible in their reality: heart and its pathways.

For a moment I was lifted out of that scene. The world
around me disappeared, and nothing existed in the universe
for me except that vibrant red instant of complex life pro-
ceeding, though doomed, with astonishing trust. The miracle of it, a hallowed miracle. Who could think otherwise?
"A mouse is miracle enough to stagger sextillion infidels."
Whitman, again. And I agree.

I've often experienced a moment of deep happiness when
watching someone sleeping, and wondered why. I think
what occasions that joy is an awareness of the truth that the
body itself is totally innocent, flesh and bone unquestion-
ably fine, justified, and without blame. All aspects—feet
and legs, the intricacy of the ears, the grace of the neck and
the arms—are sculptures unsurpassed in beauty of line and
function. And the hands, solely in and of themselves, are
astonishingly perfect and inviolate. Jacob Bronowski writes

in *The Ascent of Man:* "I remember as a young father tiptoe-
ing to the cradle of my first daughter when she was four or
five days old and thinking, these marvelous fingers, every
joint so perfect, down to the fingernails. I could not have
designed that detail in a million years."

When the human body is sleeping we can see clearly,
without interference or confusion, that the body is indeed
sacred and honorable—a grand gift we hold in trust. It is
sublime and chaste in its loveliness and as unbothered by
greed or violence, by deceit or guilt, as a brilliantly yellow
cottonwood standing in an autumn field, as the moon fill-
ing the boundaries of its white stone place. If there is sin,
it resides elsewhere. "The man's body is sacred and the
woman's body is sacred," wrote Whitman.

The world provides every physical image and sensation
we will ever need in order to experience the sacred, to
declare the holy. If we could only learn to recognize it, if
we could only hone and refine our sense of the divine, just
as we learn to see and distinguish with accuracy the ant on
the trunk of the poplar, the Pole Star in Ursa Minor, rain
coming toward us on the wind; just as we come to identify
the sounds we hear, the voices of our children, the creak of
the floor at the lover's footstep, the call of a finch unseen
in the top of a pine; just as we can detect and name the
scent of cedar or lilac, wild strawberries, or river mud and
rotting logs.

Might it be possible, if we try, to become so attuned to
the divine that we are able to perceive and announce it with
such ease too? And perhaps the divine, the sacred, the holy,

only come into complete existence through our witness of them, our witness for them and to them. If this is so, then our obligations are mighty and humbling. We are co-creators. We are servants.

I believe we move through the sacred constantly yet remain oblivious to its presence except during those rare, unexpected moments when we are suddenly shocked and shaken awake, compelled to perceive and acknowledge. During those brief moments we know with bone-centered conviction who it is we are; with breath-and-pulse clarity where it is we have come from; and with earth-solid certainty we know to what it is we owe all our allegiance, all our heart, all our soul, all our love.

(1998)

# "I Hear and Behold God in Every Object, Yet Understand God Not in the Least"

"For God so loved the order of things that he gave his only begotten son that whosoever believes in him should not perish. . . ." So Jesus said, according to John. God so loved the world, loved the order of things, loved the earth, loved the order of the earth, loved us as creatures born of the order of things, born of the stars and the order of the stars, born of the earth born of the stars, made of the stars, made of the earth. I fall into the beauty of that song and momentarily I am saved. I do not perish. I agree with Walt Whitman: "I hear and behold God in every object, yet understand God not in the least."

Maybe the creative order of the universe—those massive stars, the supernovas, those super stars smelting in their nuclear furnaces all the elements from which every body in the universe is composed, the planets gathering those elements to become themselves, the earth slowly forming, core and mantle, mountains rising, tectonic plates shifting, the great oceans of the earth churning for billions of years until the first flickering grip of life begins, those first, daring, determined, primordial creatures coming and coming—maybe the processes of this order resulted ultimately in the birth of a certain child who came to be called the Christ. Perhaps the universe brought forth in love this child who uttered those words. Maybe this was the way it happened—the order of things, the universe, the love embodied in creation bringing forth this fruit.

I don't know how it happened. But here it is, our earth and the heavens, those words, the story of that life, that resounding message. And isn't it true that love enhances, gives health and energy, causes the capacity for good to expand, is kin to joy, a cousin to reverence, while hate hinders, withers its host, promotes destruction, brings anger and misery, nurtures the well-being of nothing? Love is a creative force in the physical world. We are agents of love and its witnesses.

Jesus Christ could not have lived without love, the Christ story could never have been conceived by anyone without love, the words themselves would never have existed without love, and without the words and a speaker of words this story could not have been told. *God is love.* He is said to have said. Maybe love was what was there before the beginning, before the Big Bang. Maybe love is the creative power within the order of things. Maybe love is the way of the universe. I could take the beauty of that into my heart.

"Consider the lilies of the field, how they grow: they neither toil nor spin, and yet I say to you that even Solomon in all his glory was not arrayed like one of these." Those words of beauty were placed in their order by a poet in love with the earth. "Not one sparrow falls to the ground that God is not aware." Those words of honor were composed by a poet in love with the life of the earth. "The meek shall inherit the earth." Who better to receive with love the order of the earth? Maybe a child born of love who then loves wholly, purely, perfectly, with all his heart and all his soul and all his mind can walk on water, can give sight to the blind, can rise again from the dead, can be this attuned with the creative love within the order of things. That child, the gift of the universe, would be love in human form. Maybe this is how love conceived itself.

I am in love with the life of the earth, the hundred budding eyes seeking light in a water-buried nest of tadpoles, a tomato on the vine basking from blossom to ripe red, in love with our enormous, frightening sun and all creatures basking in the light of its being, a green anole invisible on a green leaf, a yellow-striped garter snake curled on a smooth stone, in love with the fragrance of a river when a summer evening begins to cool and the cicadas and crickets strike up their buzz and jingle in the poplars and shore grasses. I'm in love with the cosmic heaven, its terrible, haunting glory, its racing explosions and dangerous maelstroms of burning rocks and dusts and great arcs of glowing gases, in love with the silence of that same sky above midnight snow, the white land and its barren shadows drenched in the pale blue stillness of the moon; in love with the order of things, crystals adhering piece by icy piece, a single, widening furl of campfire smoke, electrons and atoms, ocean currents and the rhythmic currents of blood through the bodies of living creatures and the rhythmic currents and waves of a veering flock of ricebirds over the fields, the sweep of porpoises veering through the swell of ocean waves; and our own creations, the written language of musical scores, bells and drums, wax whistles and pianos, hot air balloons, bicycles, rollerblades, calculus, arboretums, *Voyager I* and *Voyager II*, and all voyagers traveling to the constant night of the ocean floors or to the airless glacier peaks of mountains or into the realms of the nano world, actors, artists, acrobats, archivists, a quilt spread on the grass, supper on a quilt spread on the grass, in love with our words alone in an otherwise wordless universe (as far as we know), in love with *as far as we know*, in love with *amen*.

All of us want to be loved unconditionally. We crave that love. We are born craving to be loved unconditionally. Some of us become warped and crippled from the lack of that love, some of us become stunted, some of us sicken, some of us die from the lack of that love. Maybe the health and vibrancy of the universe too depends on a love like that. Maybe the creation is not finished. Maybe the creation, in its ongoing shifting and changing, altering and evolving, requires a robust strength that love alone can provide, a love given freely and unconditionally throughout the coming and going of stars and mountains and suns and planets, in the coming and going of life. We know we are a source of love. We know we have the ability to receive and to give love, to sustain by giving love. We can love the order of the world, receive and acknowledge with love its gifts of life and beauty and one another. We can express love to a universe that requires it, give love despite fear, despite horror and

grief, despite suffering, despite our ignorance, love unconditionally despite death. Each of us can give that gift as we
are able. I want this gift to be received. I want to participate
in the creation in this way now, wherever now might be, in
place, in time, among the countless and the far beyond.

(2008)

( PART IV )

# An Interview with Richard McCann

*(This interview was derived from nine hours of tapes recorded in Houston, Texas, August 1985.)*

I

Straight up away from this road,
Away from the fitted particles of frost
Coating the hull of each chickpea,
And the stiff archer bug making its way
In the morning dark, toe hair by toe hair,
Up the stem of the trillium,
Straight up through the sky above this road right now,
The galaxies of the Cygnus A cluster
Are colliding with each other in a massive swarm
Of interpenetrating and exploding catastrophes.
I try to remember that.

(from "Achieving Perspective")

*Richard McCann:* One of the surprising qualities of your first book, *The Expectations of Light*, was, as Peter Stitt noted in the *Georgia Review*, "its sophisticated incorporation of modern scientific thinking into poetry." Did you consciously set out to incorporate the findings and vocabulary of contemporary science into your poetry?

*Pattiann Rogers:* I didn't have a formulated way of looking at life that I wanted to express in poetry. The poetry has created me at the same time that I was creating the poetry, especially over the last five to seven years. There is one thing I did consciously try to accomplish, however, and I worked on it for a number of years, and that was to find some way of incorporating into my poetry the massive scientific vocabulary that has built up. This vocabulary has been mainly an untapped vocabulary, and many of the words are very evocative, not sterile at all. But I didn't only want to be able to use this vocabulary. I wanted to express the kind of wonder and exhilaration that I felt was contained in much of what science has been discovering and also to reflect in my poetry how some of these discoveries affect our ways of seeing ourselves. I felt that somehow poetry was going to have to deal with the process of science and what science is saying. Poetry could not pretend science was not radically changing our basic concepts about ourselves. We are the poets of the latter half of the twentieth century. How could we, the verbal interpreters of our age, ignore science? Or even worse, deal with it out of fear or anger?

*RM:* In what ways did you want to deal with science's impact?

*PR:* This was a conscious intent I had: to employ scientific vocabulary to the extent I was able and to employ it in a way that would convey some of my own enthusiasm for what science was telling us and to use that vocabulary as an investigative tool to discover and at the same time shape some of my own feelings; I wanted to work toward discovering, through my poetry, how what science is saying—about origins and development of life and the universe, about the ultimate particle, about space and time and matter and light and perception—how all of these affect our visions.

I kept trying to do this, but I couldn't find the right approach; the poems were no good. Around this time, or a little before, I read an essay, "The Value of Science," by Richard P. Feynman, a well-known physicist. He wrote:

> I stand at the seashore, alone, and start to think. There are rushing waves . . . mountains of molecules, each stupidly minding its own business . . . trillions apart . . . yet forming white surf in unison. Ages on ages . . . before any eyes could see . . . year after year . . . thunderously pounding the shore as now. For whom for what? . . . on a dead planet, with no life to entertain.

In other words, he's thinking poetic things—and what he's thinking and feeling is based on what science has revealed about the development of Earth and man, about matter and atoms, about how molecules work in a wave. He wrote:

> The same thrill, the same awe and mystery, come again and again when we look at any problem deeply enough. With more knowledge comes deeper, more wonderful mystery, luring one on to penetrate deeper still. . . . It is true that few unscientific people have this particular type of religious experience. Our poets do not write about it; our artists do not try to portray this remarkable thing. I don't know why.

Is nobody inspired by our present picture of the universe? The value of science remains unsung by singers, so you are reduced to hearing, not a song or a poem, but an evening lecture about it. This is not yet a scientific age.

This just struck me like a thunderbolt. Why can't we sing about this? And then I thought—here is a scientist who wants the artist. He's a scientist. He's doing his work in the way he must, and he feels incomplete and distressed because his exhilaration, his religious feeling about the universe, is not being expressed—as he wants it to be expressed—by those best able to express it in a meaningful, artistic way. It seemed a kind of plea to me, a cry. It made me even more determined to keep working at what I was trying to do.

RM: When did you first begin to feel successful in these attempts?

PR: "The Rites of Passage" comes first to my mind now. I couldn't believe it as I began to feel this poem coming into shape; I couldn't believe it. Did I do it this time? But accomplishing it in this poem didn't mean I could do it again. I had many subsequent failures. But doing it right once meant I knew what it felt like to do it right. I've always felt that if I could do just a little bit, that if I could make that crack, that opening, there might be poets coming after me who could do this better than I have done it. I'm not a scientist. I want that always clearly understood. I understand certain things in science, but I'm not a physicist. I'm not a zoologist. I'm not a botanist. I'm not an astronomer. Sometimes I know where to go to look for information I need, but I hope there will be other poets more knowledgeable than I am who will do this is in their own ways.

*RM:* But you studied science as an undergraduate at the University of Missouri, majoring in English literature and minoring in zoology; and your husband is a geophysicist. How has physics—the work of Heisenberg and Einstein, for example—been important to your poetry? In *The Tattooed Lady in the Garden* you cite Heisenberg: "What we observe is not nature itself but nature exposed to our method of questioning."

*PR:* Trying to discuss the new roles of physics is like poetry. Niels Bohr, speaking to Heisenberg, is recorded as saying, "When it comes to atoms, language can be used only as in poetry. The poet, too, is not nearly so concerned with describing facts as with creating images." Einstein used to say a scientist is like a seamstress who makes a coat and holds it up to see if it fits the universe or not. If it doesn't fit, he takes it back to the workshop and works on it some more. My work is an ongoing investigation too, in a sense— each poem is an investigation in itself, and whatever the work comes to mean as a whole is an investigation with discoveries made along the way.

*RM:* In your poem "Reaching the Audience," which investigates the many ways of seeing by which one might know an iris, you call your work "these volumes-in-progress," which, in some ways, recalls Whitman's ever-expanding *Leaves of Grass*. Does the sense of your work as "volumes-in-progress," as "an investigation with discoveries made along the way," affect the ways in which you arrange that work within individual volumes?

*PR:* It's hard for me to break the work up into books. Books require that I make a linear arrangement of my work. That's what the publishing company demands; it has to be done. But it's so arbitrary in a way. Why should one poem have to follow another and why should one poem be the beginning and another be the ending? That's not my vision of my work at all. I envision my work as being interrelated and circular. I made a joke about this once at a reading. I said that I think the perfect book would be a clear plastic, inflatable ball. The poems would be printed on the surface of that globe, so that when you read any single poem, you would see it surrounded by other poems, and you would see other poems behind it. Each time you would turn the globe, there would be new configurations. My poems don't seem to be separate entities. One poem may give rise to three or four others; a question will rise from writing one poem, and that question becomes another poem, which in turn gives rise to yet other poems.

*RM:* Given your interest in science, what brought you to, and what keeps you with, the specific medium of poetry?

*PR:* Some people seem to be curious as to why anyone would write poetry when it seems so few read it. A few years before we had the space shuttle, I heard a professor from M.I.T. being interviewed on a television program outlining the future plans of our space program. He was saying that he wanted to make space travel available to people other than

astronauts. He said, "My goal is to be able to take a poet
to the first space station." Whether he read poetry or not,
it seemed to me that there was an unquestioned assumption
on his part that there were poets working. It seemed to me
that this man, like Feynman, expected that the work he was
engaged in would somehow be experienced and investigated
by someone who could express the glory and beauty and
awe of it, who could invest it with a purpose beyond its
physical accomplishment. It seemed unquestioned, accepted
that this person would be a poet.

*RM:* If you were chosen to be that poet on the first space
station, what would your role be? How would you begin
the poem?

*PR:* I wrote a poem about this, "NASA Takes a 63-year-old
Poet to the First Space Station." It's in the last section of *The
Expectations of Light.* It isn't written from my viewpoint on the
space station, however; but the way I would begin a poem
like that would be the way I begin any poem. I would start
with the senses, and I would start with my sensual pleasure
in what I was experiencing; or I would describe a physical object very carefully and then see if anything else rose
out of that. That to me is the salvation. Salvation is in the
physical object, whether it's my body, a locust, an egret, an
iris, or a man-made object in space. In the particular physical object lies all that I discover. I would try to describe that
in the finest words I could find, in exact words, in words
that fit. Like the scientist holding up a garment to see if it
fits the universe, I would try to write so that I could hold

that poem up, and it would fit my feelings, and yet, oddly enough, create my feelings at the same time.

II

Suppose benevolent praise,
Coming into being by our will,
Had a separate existence, its purple or azure light
Gathering in the upper reaches, affecting
The aura of morning haze over autumn fields,
Or causing a perturbation in the mode of an asteroid.
What if praise and its emanations
Were necessary catalysts to the harmonious
Expansion of the void? Suppose, for the prosperous
Welfare of the universe, there were an element
Of need involved?

(from "Supposition")

RM: What unifies the scientist's way-of-seeing and the artist's way-of-seeing?

PR: I think science is a form of investigation; so is art. "Let's investigate this man's face," an artist says. "And we'll do it with oils on canvas." Or Schubert says, "I want to investigate trout, so I'll write a quintet." It's the activity or process of the investigation that has value, not necessarily the results. We all have a desire to capture something absolutely. We want to cling to some certainty, all of us. But we live in a world of flux, and I think that fluctuation itself is a pleasure. Do we really want something that's known with certainty? Do we really want that? I don't know. I think we enjoy the process of constantly discovering things, surprising ourselves, having this wonderful, infinite puzzle to work on. And what kind of mystery would it be if we could solve it anyway? Investigating this mystery—whether the investigation is done by electron microscope or violin or calculus or ballet—is an activity of praise and adoration and affirmation.

RM: How is science an activity of praise?

PR: Stephen Jay Gould, a biologist, studies a particular type of rare snail that only lives on a single island somewhere. He adores that work. He has said something to the effect that he doesn't care if there are only seven other people in the world who are interested in what he discovers about the snail. Every time he discovers something about the life of that snail that was never known before, he feels a tremendous exhilaration and a sense of success. I think that's a high form of reverence and praise.

RM: How is that praise? Is it the thing being praised, or the activity?

PR: Praise is an activity. That's a high honor to pay a snail— for someone to spend his whole life finding out everything he can about how it lives and how it survives, how it endures. Indifference is a kind of death, a condemnation to death. And what is even more wonderful is that the study of that snail can last a whole lifetime and longer! It isn't a narrow, restricted study. Study the snail long enough and the whole universe can be seen there. That wasn't my idea: "a world in a grain of sand." That's why I come back to the word "praise"; it's the only thing I know we can do safely and assuredly. I know we can do that. We can invent our songs and we can sing. There's not a doubt in the world we can do that, and I think it's important that we do it.

*RM:* But isn't the scientist at least conceived of as attempting to know some absolute, as attempting to take the world and pin it down?

*PR:* I think that's not right about scientists. I don't think scientists lock things in. Their body of knowledge is very flexible, constantly being refined as their techniques and instruments become more refined. Dogmas—political and religious—claim certainty, not science. Scientists nearly always use qualifiers when announcing the results of their work. Neither the artist nor the scientist captures an absolute certainty. We don't ask the artist to do that, but for some reason the scientist is expected to do that whether or not he even believes it is possible. I think if ever the ultimate answer to the mystery of the universe were found, the scientists would be the most disappointed people around. They love the mystery; they love the puzzle of it all, and they love trying to solve that puzzle. It is a popular misconception, I think, that the scientist is after an absolute certainty. It was Heisenberg, after all, who developed the Uncertainty Principle.

*RM:* Do you know Whitman's poem, "When I Heard the Learn'd Astronomer"? Despite everything Whitman says about the value of science to poetry in his 1855 preface to *Leaves of Grass,* in "When I Heard the Learn'd Astronomer," the astronomer's evening lecture reduces Whitman's experience of the universe, and his sense of wonder is not restored until he leaves the auditorium and wanders in silence beneath the actual stars.

*PR:* I wish so much that when Whitman went out in silence he was awed by what he could know about the universe, but I don't think that's what he means. He means that the figures, the columns, and the charts were still a distraction from actual experience. I had an astronomy class at the University of Missouri that profoundly affected me. I had exactly the opposite reaction from Whitman. I was awestruck with revelation as to what was up there in the heavens. I was also struck not only by what I was discovering about the complexity and size of the universe, but also by what a marvelous wonder it was that we could know and discover these things. I was not even aware that we could know such things. I had feelings of tremendous release and power and possibility that this earth was not all that there was, and that I was not confined here. What science tells us is often liberating.

*RM:* Perhaps poetry's distrust of science originates in the early part of the twentieth century, during World War I, with the sorts of anti-technological views that Hart Crane felt called up to answer in *The Bridge.* When considering nuclear weaponry, however, it is difficult to conceive of science as being "an activity of praise, adoration, and affirmation."

*PR:* Technology and science are sometimes confused in people's minds; technology rises from pure science. What scientists discovered about the nature of the atom made the technology of nuclear weapons possible. And, well, I think it's been impressed on all of us quite strongly that we are fallible beings, and that mankind as a species is brutish and bestial (I don't mean to cast a bad reflection on the beasts). There are many voices in our society proclaiming this fact over and over. So what do we do? We know these things about ourselves. The question is what to do about them. I guess I agree with Faulkner that the poet's duty, his privilege, is "to help man endure by lifting his heart, by reminding him of the courage and honor and hope and pride and compassion and pity and sacrifice which have been the glory of his past." So when I speak of science, I mean to refer not only to the discoveries science has made but also to the process of science. And I mean to refer to the best that science has offered us and to the best scientists, just as when we speak of American literature we mean to refer to the best literary works that we have produced. I think our finest scientists have a very great respect for the world, nature, and the universe, and that they feel a reverence for it.

*RM:* In *The Tattooed Lady in the Garden*, our human relationship to the natural world seems far more hopeful than in some of the works of your predecessors and contemporaries, in which "human life" seems antithetical to and hostile toward "natural life" and in which human language serves primarily as a justification for murderous human behavior. I'm thinking, for instance, of W. S. Merwin's "For a Coming Extinction," in which the speaker tells the gray whale "That we who follow you invented forgiveness / and forgive nothing," or in Merwin's "Avoiding News by the River," in which the natural landscape "fills with blood" as human life awakens. How do you see humans—with our language, particularly—as sustaining the natural world?

*PR:* I have this sense of an ongoing creation, and that we are part of it, and to separate ourselves as merely observers of the universe is a big error. We have been a part of it; we are right in the middle of the universe, not only being an effect but also affecting this ongoing process. I think a poem that deals with this is "Supposition": "Suppose the molecular changes taking place / in the mind during an act of praise / resulted in an emanation rising into space. . . . "

*RM:* This seems to me to be the first real appearance in *The Expectations of Light* of a theme that is to become major in *The Tattooed Lady in the Garden*. The working title of *The Tattooed Lady in the Garden*, for instance, was "The Dimension of Witness"; the act of witnessing is central to these poems.

*PR:* As I was working on "Supposition" and on similar poems, I had this thought: What if we are the only cognitive beings in the universe? What if we are the only creatures with self-awareness? Then what part in the ongoing creation of the universe does our witnessing play—I used this religious word, "witnessing"—if we are the creatures solely responsible for these activities? I don't know the answer; just the question itself brings forth so much. At one time I thought: if we don't name the stars they will never be named. How terrible, the poor stars never to be distinguished. That's our gift, our talent. We can bestow that kind of distinction—

that kind of reality and being—on the universe. Fred Wolfe, in the introduction to his book *Taking the Quantum Leap*, says, "Quantum mechanics appears to describe a universal order that includes us in a very special way. In fact, our minds may enter into nature in a way we had not imagined possible. The thought that atoms may not exist without observers of atoms is, to me, a very exciting thought." That's a tremendously exciting thought to me, too!

RM: Is it possible we name the stars in order to distinguish ourselves, not to distinguish them? Can't the act of naming be a way of finishing them off?

PR: Some people do consider that once a thing is given a name it can be set aside. I don't believe that. I think the poem "How the Moon Becomes Itself" addresses that question. A curious mind doesn't let the name be the end of the process of knowing; it is part of the process. I think that our language has locked us into this idea that something has got to be one thing or the other, that it can't be two or even more things at once. Why can't one thing be an infinite variety of things and not be contradictory to itself? We see ourselves as an accumulation of contradictions and yet we accept ourselves as being a whole unit. Poets must work all of the time to overcome the limitations of language. An object can be two contradictory things or two things that seem contradictory.

RM: Language then does not separate us from the creation?

PR: Helen Keller's testimony of the discovery of language is so important: she is one of the few people who could say what it was like to live without language. Some people think that's a desirable state to move toward, but I think Keller's testimony says just the opposite. The world for her was not created until she learned language; at that moment, the world became real for her. I think it was that moment of discovering what language was that sustained her for the rest of her life; if you have ever seen a picture of her even as an old woman, you see joy all over her face. Before she knew what language was, she was a completely selfish human being; she felt no guilt, no remorse, no love; she only ran to her mother for protection, not with affection; she was ungenerous, unthankful. But her teacher's diary says that the moment Helen Keller had the revelation that everything had a name, her face completely changed to a glow, and it began to be expressive in a way it had never been before. You must remember that even before this she had a small vocabulary, primarily signals. What she lacked was a *language*, a means by which she could investigate the world, nurture the world, affirm the world. Her teacher said that Keller crawled into her lap that night and kissed her good night and patted her face. What we might call spirituality entered Keller at that moment.

RM: In *The Tattooed Lady in the Garden*, the repeated activities of seeing, naming, and praising seem to be activities that create the universe; in the poem "Angel of the Atom," for instance, reality is created by perceiving and naming it. Yet you describe the "angel" who is within each atom as "real but nonexistent," as a "real illusion." Is the universe a creation made by language only?

*PR:* We can give meaning to the universe. I have moments of despair. I say, "This is senseless. There's no meaning to our existence at all. This is a horrible joke. We are creatures who happen by accident to be conscious of ourselves, to be conscious of where we are, and, most horribly, conscious of our own death. Our own death! This is a nightmare. How could this have happened? There's no meaning in the universe." My husband once said, "You forget that we are part of the universe, and if we give meaning to it, there is meaning in it. We are the agent of that meaning, and maybe we are the only source of that meaning."

*RM:* In "Angel of the Atom," then, the fact that we perceive, name, and therefore create meaning does not diminish that meaning's reality?

*PR:* Right, that's the dream that is the reality in "Angel of the Atom." That dream, the meaning we invent, is physical, rooted in our bones, integral to our blood and flesh, one with the material of the universe. If we deny this, we throw away the significance of what we are, what makes us human, and what we are able to contribute to the universe. Our bestowal of meaning is part of the universe, and it is real. That's what "Angel of the Atom" is about and part of what "Inside God's Eye" is about.

*RM:* At the end of "Inside God's Eye," you write, "We are the vessel and the blood / And the pulse he sees as he sees the eye watching / The vision inside his eye in the perfect mirror / Held constantly before his face." Is our role in the creation, then, to help create it through our acts of witnessing and praising?

*PR:* We are the only source for this self-awareness and maybe this is the only way god can see himself. See how our language limits me, how I have to speak this way in which all of a sudden god becomes this contained thing. I don't mean it this way, but it's the only way I can say it here and now.

*RM:* Does this "ongoing creation" include the creation of a god, as in the poem "The Creation of the Inaudible"?

*PR:* Right. The crucial stanza in that poem—for me, anyway—is the next to last stanza, in which the sound of god's being is described: "Someone far away must be saying right now / The only unique sound of his being / Is the spoken postulation of his unheard presence." That's the stanza of revelation for me, a revelation that we are in some way involved in the process of creating god, that he is not a god who has created us and put us here, but that this creation is an interaction. He becomes as we create him; he is not omnipotent, and he depends on us to complete his creation. I'm not promoting this as a doctrine; it's the idea I'm working with.

III

How can he stand to comprehend the hard, pitiful
Unrelenting cycles of coitus, ovipositors, sperm and zygotes,
The repeated unions and dissolutions over and over,
The constant tenacious burying and covering and hiding
And nesting, the furious nurturing of eggs, the bright
Breaking-forth and the inevitable cold blowing-away?
Think of the million million dried stems of decaying
Dragonflies, the thousand thousand leather cavities
Of old toads, the mounds of cows' teeth, the tufts

Of torn fur, the contorted eyes, the broken feet,
Bloated odors, the fecund brown-haired mildews
That are the residue of his process. How can he tolerate
       knowing
There is nothing else here on earth as bright and salty
As blood spilled in the open?

Maybe he wakes periodically at night,
Wiping away the tears he doesn't know
He has cried in his sleep, not having had time yet to tell
Himself precisely how it is he must mourn, not having had
       time yet
To elicit from his creation its invention
Of his own solace.

(from "The Possible Suffering of a God during Creation")


*RM:* Comparing *The Expectations of Light* to *The Tattooed Lady in the Garden*, it seems that the question of god becomes more important within your work.

*PR:* My original intention was to express what I find exhilarating about some of the things science is telling us about ourselves and to investigate by language and to praise. Those were conscious intents, but in attempting to do that, the work moved in ways I didn't expect. For one thing, I never intended to approach god as a subject and yet it is appearing more and more. The movement has been gradual and natural, at least from my standpoint.

*RM:* Specifically, how did this movement occur for you?

*PR:* My background is kind of unusual. Until I was thirteen, my family was traditionally Presbyterian and very active in the church, not just casually. When I was thirteen, my parents made a radical shift in their religious viewpoint. It came about from my father having met a man who belonged to a very small religious sect. This sect read the Bible literally and was very staunch in its beliefs, similar in ways to the Jehovah's Witnesses—very doctrinal.

*RM:* You've spoken of your father often these past two days.

*PR:* He only had an eighth-grade education, but he was tremendously creative, always tinkering with something. His big goal was to make his first million dollars; yet I don't think he wanted that at all. He just liked the idea of inventing. He invented a baseball pitching machine, which he sold to the miniature golf course. He didn't get a patent on it. He invented using light meters that would automatically dim car headlights, but he didn't get a patent on it. He invented stuff to put on the bottom of ice cube trays so they wouldn't stick to the freezer, and then we got all the kids in the neighborhood and we worked like an assembly line. He was a dynamic, energetic, optimistic man who had a lot of crazy mottoes.

*RM:* What happened when your father became involved with the religious sect?

*PR:* My father made a break with the Presbyterian church. He didn't just leave; he had to go and confront the minister, who was also a close personal friend. This was a major crisis in our family: it meant the overthrow of all kinds of social norms, and things that had been previously promoted were now regarded as evil. Until I left for college, there was a long period when religion was the subject in the house, when the Bible was read continually, and when I was taken through studies and all kinds of doctrinal arguments. When people formulate doctrines, they begin to get into arguments: there were many heated arguments. It was a stimulating and exciting time—in a terrifying way— because I did have a strange fascination and pleasure in the debates that went on. It was a sense of questioning what had been unquestioned in my life up until then, although this questioning was not always done with an intent to find truth. I was at an impressionable age; some of these questions we considered at that time have been with me since. Of course, this religion wasn't satisfactory to me. After I went to college and other questions arose, it seemed very narrow. Things like reading a novel were considered wrong because it was not God's word; reading a novel was not meditating upon God's word.

RM: Did your college experience call into question the sort of absolutism you're describing?

PR: I had a humanities course that lasted two semesters, taught by teachers from the departments of English, philosophy, and art. The philosophy part was very moving and important to me because I saw people working with language and words in order to try and explain to themselves what "I" was, and what was outside, and what was inside. It was a careful and intellectual scrutiny of language and the ways words were used, the definitions attached to words, and the kinds of things we take for granted until we hear someone question them. Meeting my husband was important. He was a physicist. He has a Ph.D. in physics and did postdoctoral work in geology.

*RM:* In college, you began to study science. How did you react to the scientists you first met?

*PR:* The process of science represented a new attitude for me, because I saw people who were not intent upon convincing somebody else of something they believed in, but who were engaged in an objective investigation to try to find out what could be known about the universe. I'm talking about scientists now. They were willing to correct themselves if they made mistakes; they were willing to change—again, we are talking about the best of science, the real scientists—and their aim was to discover what they could about nature. I liked that. It seemed important to me. It seemed right somehow; it seemed to lack a kind of pride and arrogance that goes with certain kinds of religious and political beliefs.

*RM:* Your description of poetry as mounting tentative "investigations" also seems to lack that kind of religious "pride and arrogance."

*PR:* When I was a teenager, there were lots of verses quoted about my missionary obligation to present "Truth" to others. I was constantly put in embarrassing situations in order to fulfill what, according to this religion, Christ had asked of me. I had to present my beliefs to others. I couldn't just develop a casual relationship with someone; it was my obligation to bring this kind of "Truth" to their minds.

*RM:* And so this experience affected your sense of poetry as a way of speaking that is not written in stone. . . .

*PR:* I think it's a reaction to that experience. I don't ever want my work to be considered a philosophical system. Sometimes the words and tone involved in discussing it, even in this interview, words used by me now, seem to contain an underlying assumption of closed doctrine. Niels Bohr, it is said, would always begin his lecture courses by saying, "Every sentence I utter should be regarded by you not as an assertion but as a question." I love that, and that's the attitude I want to maintain in my own work and in my comments regarding it. I think I can maintain that kind of attitude in my poetry. I hope I do. I think it's less easy to keep that tone out of this conversation. Language in a conversation like this seems to lend itself to statements that sound as if they were in concrete. I don't ever want any kind of dogma attached to what I have to say. That's one reason I write poetry. It allows the kind of flexibility of language that I love.

*RM:* Despite the prohibitions, were you reading novels and imaginative literature?

*PR:* I did, but not to the degree I would have had I been encouraged. I was isolated from my peers. The normal kinds of things teenagers do, like going to football games, were considered wrong. If I went out with a boy, I couldn't go out with him very long without attempting to convert him, because he was of the world and not of the "Truth."

*RM:* In your work, particularly in your praise of the physical world, "the world" and "Truth" never seem opposed to one another.

PR: After I left home and went to school, there was no way anybody was going to tell me that the kind of beauty I was reading in good literature or hearing in fine music was sinful. There was no way anyone was going to convince me of that. In fact, I once said to my husband, "Wouldn't it be wonderful if all god wanted from us was to create beauty? If this was all he wanted. If he didn't want us turning away from everything." Pure Christianity can be interpreted as a denial of life here on Earth because one must set one's sights on the life to come.

RM: Much of your work rises from and celebrates life here on Earth; and much of your poetry celebrates the body. . . .

PR: How beautiful the relationship between our bodies and the universe is! If I could have designed my own creation, I couldn't have thought of anything more perfect. To begin with, we are made from the dust of old stars. What could be more wonderful than that? All the elements of our bodies came from the dust of old stars. Then every once in a while I have a vision that this world is our whole history. All we have to do is look at it. It's our genealogy, our ancestry, and it's visible, right in front of us all the time, the whole thing. The same math that describes the working of the atoms in our brains describes the working of the stars in the heavens. How could we feel alone or isolated or solitary seeing that we have risen up right out of the surge of the sea, right out of the soil, out of the roots of trees, right through the skeletons and bones and blood of fish and birds and bears? The human embryo passes through many of these stages in its development. And the very atoms that compose our bodies have already traveled through the dark reaches of space. Sometimes I feel like the universe is just waiting for us to accept ourselves. We don't know how to do it yet.

*RM:* In "The Reincarnated" and "The Rites of Passage," the body becomes a way of knowing, as though it might recall vast histories that we have forgotten. In "The Rites of Passage," for instance, you conclude your description of the birth of the frog eggs by describing your reaction to this event:

> Think of that part of me wishing to remember
> The split-second edge before the beginning,
> To remember by a sudden white involution of sight,
> By a vision of tension folding itself
> Inside clear open waters, by imitating a manipulation
> Of cells in a moment of distinction, wishing to remember
> The entire language made during that crossing.

What is it you encourage the body to "remember"?

*PR:* I have a feeling that we know many things, that our bodies respond to things that we haven't been able to verbalize yet. So, in a sense, we don't know them. We can't investigate them because we need to have them in language in order to look at them and examine them. It is in this sense that I use the word "remember." There are too many strange things going on. We have these vague words like "intuition," "feeling," "sense," and "music." What is music? What in the world is that? Our bodies can tell us things. Sometimes we "know" when the garment has been made right, if it fits right, or if something seems true, we have a certain feeling about it. Where does that feeling come from? It's a bodily feeling, not an abstraction. I tried to approach the subject in "Capturing the Scene." I think we have to do everything we can with our minds. We have to work to our potential in analyzing, in naming, in taking apart, investigating by using the checks on superstition that science has developed, and we have to continually ask others, "Is this how you see this happening too?" And then there are the times when we put everything back together and remember something more. But all of the analysis and concentration, all of the intellectualization is what helps us make that other step in which we add our part, our humanity, what we can give. Then we see beyond the physical by means of the physical.

*RM:* Are these divisions we've been discussing—divisions between science and poetry, earth and truth, body and spirit—related to the split between knowledge and feeling? In your work, you frequently present multiple ways by which something may be seen and known.

*PR:* I think some of these divisions are locked into the language. We can't break out of that language. It forces us to think of knowledge and feeling as two separate things. Maybe there's no division there. The language forces us to think in a certain pattern, such as to think in terms of cause and effect. I have tried to break this by writing not about one thing causing another in a kind of linear fashion, but by writing about a reciprocal creation in which many things rise together, creating each other simultaneously.

*RM:* In *The Tattooed Lady in the Garden*, the real question is how to praise death.

*PR:* I like the way you're phrasing that. I think I am glad I am taking on this subject in my poetry because to ignore it would be to weaken the work as a whole. Yet there are fears I feel about some of these poems.

*RM:* What kinds of fears?

*PR:* I don't want to dramatize this. It isn't dramatic. But sometimes it happens that I've gotten into a poem and have wondered if I could get back out of it. It's kind of like a spiraling; when I'm that deep in it, I wonder if I can find my way back when I need to get back out of it. There was one poem I wrote where I was conscious of my breath for three days afterward.

*RM:* What poem was this?

*PR:* "The Possible Suffering of a God during Creation."

*RM:* What made you fearful during the writing of it?

*PR:* I can't explain it. Maybe it was those things we have been talking about—that there are crucial things that depend upon us within creation. Maybe this was the first poem where I felt impatient for whatever it is that I am calling "god," "creative force," or whatever it is. Maybe it's the first poem where I felt that he needs us, that he himself is in the process of being created, and that he needs us to complete certain aspects of his own creation.

*RM:* In many of these poems—"The Possible Suffering of a God during Creation," "The Birth Song and the Death

Song," "Trinity," "The Possible Advantages of Expendable Multitudes"—you seem to be attempting to reinvent an attitude toward death. What attitudes did you begin with that required reinvention?

*PR:* When my father died in 1975, that was the first really close death I had experienced. I still had this personal sense of god. My first reaction was that he must be an unkind god—if we're going to die, all right, but why make us aware of it? This is all a traditional view of god. Then I thought, "My father is gone, completely gone." And I thought maybe it's not god's fault, maybe he can't help it.

*RM:* It's with your father's death that the question of death first comes up in *The Expectations of Light*, in the poem "Without Violence."

*PR:* Yes, and later, in *The Tattooed Lady in the Garden*, it comes up in "The Possible Suffering of a God during Creation," with the idea that god is not perfect, that he is somehow depending on us, and that we forgive him for it. But I am still saying "him" in these old ways because I don't have another vocabulary I can use.

*RM:* In "The Rites of Passage," "life" is defined as bringing "the instantaneous distinction of being liable to death"; in "Trinity," you wonder whether death might not be "gentle," "careful," and "patient."

*PR:* "Trinity" is another example of experimenting, of saying that maybe death is like this, then. How do you reconcile being a lover of life and, at the same time, accept its inevitable conclusion? I don't know whether Dylan Thomas's

"Do Not Go Gentle into That Good Night" is the right attitude, that we should fight death all the way; or if it's like John Neihardt said, that death is like a good mother coming to you and taking you in her arms. Maybe both are right. I don't know. I am willing to try to work on it.

(1987)

# Poems That Possess Me
# Like New Music in the Blood

*An Interview with Brian Doyle*

*Brian Doyle:* What's a poem?

*Pattiann Rogers:* Jiminy! What a question to begin with! I looked up *jiminy* recently, you know—it comes from Jesu Domine. Did you know that? The word following *jiminy* is *jimjams*. I love things like that. That might answer your question.

*BD:* What starts a poem in you—a line, a phrase, a word, a smell, a note, a sight?

*PR:* All of the above, and often combinations of the above. Also music. Most classical music, and sometimes music I knew early in my life, seems like a miracle to me—the fact that there should be such a thing as making small black marks on paper in one century that can be read and translated into combinations of sounds and rhythms by someone, some stranger, in another century, and that these sounds can communicate something essential to us. Makes me proud to be human.

Sometimes visual art, usually some quirky thing that attracts my attention, can be the beginning of a poem, sometimes not even especially good visual art. A new poem, "The Background Beyond the Background," began with a picture I saw on a wall in a hotel where I stayed one night. It was the juxtaposition of the objects in the picture that attracted my attention, but the poem is not at all about the picture or the hotel room, and none of the objects in the picture is in the poem.

Maybe what all the origins of my poems have in common is that each triggers a new perspective for me, a perspective in which I see myself, and human life, differently, from afar, as if I had backed away from myself somehow. It could be that I suddenly glimpse myself against the broad expanse of human history, or against the vast particulars of the universe perhaps, or newly against the thought of God or time or death or all life in the present and all life that has disappeared, or glimpse a slightly new definition of myself and human life against the lives of other creatures, through the individual lives of other living beings. At the beginning, these new perceptions are so vague they aren't really there, just a strange feeling really. They are just suggestions that resonate in strange ways. I try to find those new perceptions and make them clearer and sharper through the music of language. Sometimes I can do this. Sometimes I can't.

*BD:* How many of your poems fail? Lots? Why do they fail? Are they resurrectable later? Are there some that stayed failed? How do you know they are lifeless? Can I ask more questions than that in a single breath?

*PR:* I suppose there are levels of failure, not to get too precise. But there are some poems that feel okay to me, feel good and well-made, yet they haven't possessed me. They haven't come over me and taken me away almost bodily. The poems that possess me like a new music in the blood, the poems that carry an energy I can feel in my bones, that charge me with happiness, that absolutely startle me, those are the poems that keep me writing, wanting that experience again and again. And it may take eight or ten mediocre poems—and I mean eight or ten poems of serious, hard work that are nevertheless mediocre or failures—to get to the one poem that is successful with that kind of success. It seems necessary to write the mediocre poems, to keep going even through those poems that truly fail with dullness and repetition and lack of coherence and discovery, that drum along with monotonous music, to be able to arrive again at the poem that breaks away, rising out of itself into some space of surprise and discovery.

When I am bored with a poem and don't look forward to working on it, I know it is a failure and is likely to remain a failure. Something went wrong somewhere—tone of voice, or stance of the speaker, maybe a lack of honesty I didn't recognize, maybe I was repeating myself and never broke out of the repetition; something blocked the way. I don't go back to poems that I consider failures. Many poets do. It doesn't work for me to return to them, although I believe I usually have learned something from a poem that has failed, something that will help me with the next poem.

*BD:* If you were a tree, what tree would you be?

*PR:* A wild river plum tree. Then I could be wild and newly beautiful every spring and rich with large sweet fruit that everyone desires and loves every fall and I could live by a river all year long. Besides, once someone sitting beside me on an airplane asked me where I was going; I said to a poetry conference and he said, "A plum tree conference! What's that?"

*BD:* Favorite poets? Poets you read for magic and power? Poets who moved and sparked and inspired and startled and started you in the craft?

*PR:* I believe that music was a greater influence in my childhood than literature. I played flute and piano, and my brother played violin, clarinet, and baritone horn, and my mother played piano. Someone was always practicing on some instrument at our house. And I sang in our church choir, and attended three different church services a week, all of which included singing, and I played in the school band and orchestra, and even in our all-city orchestra. I think my experience of music as a participant in it, a performer of it, rather than solely as audience, has been crucial to me as a poet.

I don't remember being especially interested in poetry as a child or teenager, although we jumped rope in rhythm to rhymes and chanted made-up nonsense words, and played games that had rules and boundaries and rhythmical sounds to them—basketball (you know that one), jacks, tennis, baseball. All these contain elements of poetry. It wasn't until I was a student at the University of Missouri that I began to be attracted to poetry as a written art, and began to try to write it myself. By that time I was also interested in science, and in the story that science was telling of the physical world. Walt Whitman came the closest to expressing my own enthrallment with the world and its immense variety of phenomena. I liked the energy of Whitman's work and the expanse of his interests and his celebratory tone, and I still like his work very much. Also Dylan Thomas's work. And I have been inspired by passages of lyrical prose by writers like William Faulkner and Flannery O'Connor. Later, I admired the work of Wallace Stevens and Theodore Roethke, especially—although, while I respect their work, I was never drawn to the confessional poets and never had a desire to write expressly autobiographical poems. Of poets working now I especially like the work of Charles Simic, and the playfulness and daring of Russell Edson.

*BD:* Is poetry the greatest art?

*PR:* Why do you ask me questions like that? Don't ask me any questions that have anything to do with superlatives. What's the meaning of "poetry"? How do you define "greatest"? What constitutes an "art"? Answer those questions yourself.

*BD:* I think poetry is the greatest literary art, yes, although the greatest art of all is music. I say poetry is insight set to music, and music is innate, the very rhythm and song of our blood, and an "art" is the human urge to craft a story in any form, a story that flashes some revelation and truth about who we are and how we live and how we might live and who we might be. If you measure the quality of art by possible stunning accomplishment and emotional power, I think that poetry at its best rises above prose and even theater and film, which can play in three dimensions; I think of Homer and Blake and Shakespeare as artists whose poetry carries like an arrow through time more than any other literature does. But of all human arts music is first, methinks, because it is most pervasive and heartful.

PR: You really did it. Music is an amazing art, to me. I love to recount to myself the number of human beings it takes, each skilled in a different area, to make possible a symphony concert. The composers, and those who copied and preserved the compositions, the instrument makers, skilled at their crafts—tubas, trumpets, timpani, woodwinds, strings—the music teachers who taught the performers, the performers who studied their instruments and practiced and rehearsed, all the builders who erected the concert hall—carpenters, electricians, etc.—the architect who designed it, the conductor who studied, who learned the language of music, the languages of all the instruments, the members of the audience who bought tickets, got dressed, came to the concert hall to be transported, to be informed, by sound, came for an experience that had nothing to do with physical survival. Most amazing. Always makes me certain absolutely without doubt that something is going on with the human species, something good.

Two heroes to me are my middle school music teacher and my son's middle school music teacher. What courage! All those twelve- and thirteen-year-old children, each with a noise-making instrument in his hands and these two enormously courageous teachers are attempting to teach them how to make music together. At my son's first sixth-grade band concert, the music teacher turned to the audience of glowing, proud parents and said, "I'm not certain what's going to happen here, but I'm just hoping that we'll all begin at the same time." It brought tears to my eyes, literally. And they did it! One step forward, in my opinion, in understanding what it means to be human.

*BD:* How tall are you?

*PR:* Tall's my middle name. Really—it's my maiden name. I was Pattiann Tall for many years. I am five feet three inches tall and am somewhat contentious and was recently called pugnacious by a friend. Lovely word, *pugnacious*. Also a friend told me once that when I get mad I sound like a jet taking off.

*BD:* Are you friends with iambic pentameter?

*PR:* Yes, I sure am—I wrote in fixed forms, including blank verse, for several years in the beginning. But I don't ask favors of it in particular very often any more. Learning to write in meter, to scan lines, thus developing an ear for syllables and accents, where they are falling and how the cadence of the language is leading the poem forward, these are important skills for any poet to possess, I believe.

*BD:* How did you begin writing essays?

*PR:* I have yet to write an essay on my own and submit it unsolicited for publication to a journal or magazine. To be perfectly honest, I can never think of a subject to write an essay about unless an editor gives me one and solicits an essay on that subject. Is that funny? I'm not familiar enough with the essay form or adept enough at it to achieve the kind of freedom that I can sometimes achieve writing poetry. It may have something to do with my imagined audience for poetry. In my imagination, that audience is not expecting from language the kind of communication that I imagine an audience for the essay is demanding. With an essay, I feel I have to *say* something, establish something, something the reader can reiterate. In a poem, I can do just about anything, and not do many things.

That sounds like there are no constraints in writing poetry, which is not true, of course. The ability to do anything means the writer has learned how to accomplish many things.

BD: If it's true, as pundits are always moaning and gnashing, that no one reads poetry, and no one buys poetry books, and the roaring wealth of new poetry goes mostly unread or read only by those dozen readers who read *Southwest Jackalope State Review* or the *Burbling Creek Review*, then how can you write poetry with such energy and pop, and how does poetry survive, and how do modern poets rise into the general consciousness, as Seamus Heaney has, and Mary Oliver maybe, and Czeslaw Milosz?

PR: Let me answer this in a roundabout fashion. For years I shrank from being called a poet. It seemed too grand a term, a name I hadn't deserved, a name I wasn't worthy of. I remember the first time I visited the Poets' Corner in Westminster Abbey. I believe it was on Charles Dickens's stone that the words "Master of the English Language" were written. How wonderful to be called "Master of the English Language"! Could I ever come close to mastering the English language? Could I ever cause it to sing for me, ever elevate it to an instrument of deliverance? I wanted to try. I had to try. I thought then and still believe the English language to be a most glorious and beautiful arrangement of sounds and meanings. I wanted to possess it in the way one might want to possess a lover, and to be possessed by it. On Dylan Thomas's stone were the last two lines from his poem "Fern Hill":

> Time held me green and dying
> Though I sang in my chains like the sea.

The courage of human beings astounds me, all of us, held by time, green and dying, aware of our deaths, aware of our chains, yet singing, each of us in our own ways. I wanted to say in my own way: Even though death, even though grief, even though deception, even though cruelty, even though pain, even though despair, we live and we declare ourselves. We curse. We extol. We sing. My way is to write poetry.

*BD:* What are you reading?

*PR:* Most recently I've read *Seven Short Novels* by Chekhov, *Northland Stories* by Jack London, *Nothing Like It in the World* by Stephen Ambrose, and *The Song of the Dodo* by David Quammen. At the moment I am reading *Guns, Germs, and*

*Steel* by Jared Diamond, which I am enjoying, although I believe some of his conclusions are shallow and not firmly established. Chet Raymo is a terrific writer with terrific subjects, and I've been reading his work recently also. Also the letters of Pliny the Younger, because I was in Italy last year and stayed for four weeks on the site of one of Pliny's villas, and I wanted to know more about him.

I want to mention two other writers I greatly admire: Italo Calvino and Sei Shonagon. *Invisible Cities* by Calvino, translated by William Weaver, is a book I've taught, a book immensely rich with intellect and lyricism and metaphor, and inspiring with the power and scope of imagination. I enjoy it more every time I read it. *The Pillow Book* by Shonagon (translated by Ivan Morris), a lady-in-waiting to the Empress Sadako in tenth-century Japan, is another book I've taught and that I return to often. The wit and energy and detail of observation in this book is exhilarating to me. Though neither of these books is poetry per se, many of the elements of poetry are present in both.

Mark Twain, of course! That man's contribution to world literature is unique and unparalleled. I am most grateful for his spirit and his stance. And speaking of Italy, his account of touring Italy in *Innocents Abroad* is highly engaging and extremely funny.

I realize that most of the writers I've mentioned are not contemporaries. I do read my contemporaries, of course, but none has influenced me to the extent these writers have. I return to the books of these writers who precede me to remind myself of the power of language and what it is possible to do with language and of the many ways language can address lasting human concerns through the passing details of the moment.

*BD:* So—did you learn Italian before you went to Italy?

*PR:* We tried, my husband and I. We had a tutor helping us for a few weeks and got absorbed in it—present perfect (which is the past in English), active and passive, transitive and intransitive, regular and irregular verbs. Wow! How did we ever learn even English in the first place? Languages are so subtle and so complex, all dependent on nuance, idiom, and very little, just enough, in the way of a dependable structure, a few rules with lots and lots of exceptions, and always evolving and changing, like a living organism. I was reminded of this all again by trying to learn even a smattering of another language, and it was very, very good for me, seeing as how I'm in the language game.

We got all mixed up, because the passive voice in structure in Italian is similar to the past structure of intransitive verbs, and we were saying things like "I was eaten by myself yesterday." I remember one morning when our tutor was telling us a little about all the various past tenses and their very subtle differences. For instance, is the speaker in the past and remembering the remote past, or is the speaker in the past remembering the present past, or is the speaker in the present remembering the past? These distinctions are not insignificant, because they shape our sense of time. So philosophy and even science are involved.

*BD:* What can poets learn from football?

PR: Well, when I lived in Houston, I learned a lot from the Houston Oilers' power forward, Earl Campbell.

BD: Good heavens, woman—he was a fullback, and a great one. Not a power forward.

PR: Well. He powered forward, didn't he? Anyway, Earl was a great inspiration to me to keep working hard and desperately at my writing even if it only meant moving the ball one more inch down the field toward the goal posts. You remember how, even when he was completely flat down with several defensive players landing on him, he was still inching that ball forward until the whistle blew.

BD: Are you a nature worshipper?

PR: No, I'm not, as I understand the word "worship."

BD: Are you leery of nature worship?

PR: Yes, I am.

BD: Are you a "nature writer"?

PR: I'm a poet who is very curious about how the physical world works and fascinated by all the various ways the various beings of the living world maintain themselves and in awe of their utter devotion to life and enthralled with the beauty of the physical world, heavens and Earth—beetle and comet, shimmy worm and dagger pod and bobolink and sun pillar—and in love with all the names of all the features of our universe, and delighted with the energy and creativity of human beings, and frightened at the harsh indifference of the physical world, and cognizant of the fact that the universe and the life of the earth at large is ruthless and without pity and without remorse and is not a model for morality, does not teach morality, and that compassion exists in the physical world because humans invented it, the same for justice and altruism and grace and mercy and praise. And I'm a poet who wants to express gratitude for the life given and the words given and for the giver, of whom I know nothing.

BD: What is God?

PR: You sure ask easy questions! I'll just talk about this a little. I certainly can't answer the question.

First, most of us have difficulty envisioning a Force of Creation outside the realm of the human in which we operate. Whether we believe in sentient spirits inhabiting all elements of the physical world or spiritual beings inhabiting the space of the heavens and stars or a voice proclaiming, "Let there be light," it's difficult not to envision these forces with bodies, faces and hands, voices that speak our words, beings with memories and plans like we have, beings that operate with intention and motives, that are either pleased or angry. These are qualities and elements with which we're familiar. These are the qualities and elements our language has evolved to address. As human creatures, wonderful as we are, our experience and knowledge of the universe is extremely limited, to say the least, and the span of time we have had, even as a species, to contemplate the dilemma of our existence and its purpose (or lack of it) has been incredibly brief. We struggle. Our brains are crude; our language is clumsy. I believe, and yet I continue to seek.

Second, I've felt for some time that the Creator or the Benevolence (for lack of a better term) within this universe is not omnipotent or omniscient, and that the universe is in the process of being created, and that we have a role to play in that process, in bringing the universe into fulfillment. We struggle to understand that role. But we have a sense, I believe, of when our actions and thoughts are healthy and strong and constructive, full of hope and affirmation, and when they are destructive, hurtful, small and withered, when they shatter others and the world around us in harmful ways, when they inhibit beauty.

I believe God or the Creator or the Benevolence is not complete, that we are needed in some way, that this benevolence needs our praise, our gratitude, our acknowledgment of all the elements of our lives and all the lives we recognize on Earth, and that we have obligations to fulfill, obligations toward the physical universe, which are not separate from the Creator, in my opinion. That duality between body and soul, flesh and spirit, is erroneous, I think. Maybe we are the consciousness of the universe, the means by which it can come to see and love itself. That's a weighty responsibility, but one I feel we can carry out.

But beliefs are always evolving, in transition, refining themselves, expanding themselves. And my poetry I see as an attempt to explore and discover, to try to come closer, millimeter by millimeter, to the heart, to try to imagine what is, what could be.

*BD:* What is the nature of forgiveness?

*PR:* Many different things. To forgive someone who hasn't asked for forgiveness is very different from forgiving someone who has asked and sought forgiveness, the first step toward repairing damage. To forgive your neighbor for having a dog that barks all night is not the same thing as forgiving your spouse for adultery. For me to forgive the Unabomber is not the same as for the mother of one of his victims to forgive him. Forgiving all mankind is not the same as forgiving the person who sits across the table from you. Forgiving yourself may be the hardest kind of forgiving, because you can't posture as being magnanimous. And what about forgiving someone who continues to commit the deed for which he has been forgiven?

*BD:* If God is all-powerful, can He make a rock so big that even He can't lift it?

*PR:* I am not a Catholic schoolboy, but I have heard that Catholic schoolboy joke many times. Nice try. I've already said I don't believe in an omnipotent creator, which addresses the paradox presented in that joke.

*BD:* What were and are the most piercing joys and penetrating pains for you about being a mother?

*PR:* Now you have really opened an enormous topic with me—my children, all children. It would take days for me to address this adequately. My two sons are now thirty-three and thirty, and that means there are many, many memories.

Being a good mother, the best mother I could manage to be as I have understood and conceived of a good mother, has

been the first and strongest and most long-lasting ambition
of my life. I still feel that being a good, dependable parent is
the most important work any of us will ever do. All of us as
adults live daily with our first childhood impressions of life
and humanity and ourselves, our self-image. How confident
we are, how bold and creative and imaginative we are, how
well we cope with failure and success, and tragedy and grief,
what we value, how capable we are of loving—all of these
capacities are determined in great part by our experiences as
children. Parents cannot control everything in a child's life,
certainly, but no one can deny the enormous effect that parents have on their children's lives and consequently on the
lives of the adults those children become and consequently
on the future of human culture and civilization. I have
never regretted the time I gave my children, and they have
returned to me gifts beyond measure, joys and understanding I would never have achieved without them.

BD: How do you pray?

PR: In a very real sense—real to me, anyway—my poems
are prayers. They're prayers that say, under their words,
"Here. I make this in praise, in confusion. I make this while
knowing nothing. Accept this, accept me." That's one kind
of poem, one kind of prayer, I think. But this is very, very
private and not public prayer. In fact, this prayer is below
the surface of the poem, invisible to others, I hope.

It may be impertinent of me, but I believe that when
human beings perform creative acts of imagination and
do so with reverence and joy, they are praying. They are

bestowing honor. They are expressing gratitude, whether they are observing the living habits of the bean clam or finding, naming, describing a butterfly or a rainforest beetle or a supernova, or sketching a wildflower, or cooking a wonderful casserole, or inventing a drug to ease suffering or a technology to aid communication, or playing Scott Joplin with verve and distinction, or dancing Prokofiev's *Romeo and Juliet,* or rolling down a hillside with abandon. Recently I happened to see a young calf jumping and leaping in a field, a common and ordinary leap for the joy of living. I felt my own joy rising while I watched it. Maybe the creator is similar, taking joy in our joy of living expressed in all the various ways human beings express joy, the way we take pleasure in our curiosity and fascination with the worlds around us. Making God happy—how audacious, how arrogant, how simpleminded I am!

BD: And, speaking of love, who was the first boy you ever kissed?

PR: Ah, you wouldn't know him. But before I go on about love, I want to say something about laughter. Kierkegaard said, "Laughter is a form of prayer." I believe that and hold to it. I've kept a small jester doll for years sitting on my desk where I write. It reminds me not to take myself too seriously. It's the jester that often opens the way to the soul. It's laughter that often takes down the veil. Poetry always has an element of playfulness about it. Good poetry moves language around in strange ways, invents new words, creates unusual juxtapositions, places words in spaces where they have never been before, and sometimes surprises itself at the results of its own whimsy.

Back to love, I will say that I was engaged twice before I was seventeen. With the second fellow, we planned to live in a rented farmhouse that had no running water, and I was going to work in a nearby shoe factory when I graduated from high school. I don't know how I escaped that future, except that I decided I didn't like him anymore because he couldn't laugh at himself and because he told me that I was too independent for a girl and my parents hadn't raised me right. Instead, I married the most intelligent, interesting, patient, devoted man I have ever known. We have interesting, stimulating conversations every single day. I'm not exaggerating. And his insights and knowledge and perspectives continue to surprise me after forty years of marriage.

*BD:* How'd you meet your husband?

*PR:* In French class as undergraduates at the University of Missouri. Our professor always handed back our test papers in order—the top grade first. John always got his paper first and I always got mine second. At the end of the semester, our professor kept us both after class and asked us if we would like to go into the advanced French class for top students. John said no, and I said yes, and then John said yes. That was the beginning.

*BD:* Should you be hired for this position, Ms. Rogers, what do you see yourself doing in five years?

*PR:* In five years, I plan, God willing, of course, to be muddling along still between the two immensities, as they say, birth and death, and to be coping in the midst of ordinary confusion and persistent mystery (though the particular confusion and mystery of today may have evolved during the intervening years and redefined itself and cast itself in slightly different tones and cadences, the music of befuddlement with a different beat but confusion and mystery all the same). And I will be recounting in lines and stanzas, to the best of my ability, my praise of the unknown and my praise of terror, and my gratitude for the tenacity of being in all its forms and implications, putting forward the best face possible on the situation in which we find ourselves, striving to maintain a faith that also evolves and falters and rights itself and redefines itself again and again.

*BD:* Do you love the human race?

*PR:* Unreservedly, despite our idiocies and crimes.

*BD:* Why?

*PR:* We're so quirky and strange and eager and creative and busy and curious and totally unpredictable and at the core innocent and ignorant and extremely interested in one another.

*BD:* What's your most deeply held spiritual belief?

*PR:* That we have responsibility for how the universe comes finally to be and for the existence of divinity.

*BD:* I think we should just leave that idea glistening there by itself and let the readers chew on it thoughtfully for a while.

(2000)

# Breaking Old Forms

*A Conversation with Gordon Johnston*

*(The following conversation took place October 24, 2005, in Pattiann Rogers's study in her home in Colorado.)*

*Gordon Johnston:* Pattiann, your eleventh and latest book of poems, *Generations* (2004), came some twenty-three years after the publication of your first. I'm wondering how you feel critics and reviewers have received the new work, and I'd also like to hear something about how you came to choose the collection's title.

*Pattiann Rogers:* What has disappointed me a little about *Generations* is that the reviews of it that I've read (with the exception of one) treat it as if it's the only book I've ever written. Nothing is mentioned about this book, my eleventh, in relation to my previous work. It's never acknowledged as the next book in a body of work, another piece of an entire vision. There's no discussion of how the work has evolved or changed or repeated previous work. As a result, the reviews, which have been very few actually, seem shallow and deficient and not particularly useful.

As to the title, I was thinking of "generations" in several different ways. I had a vision of people, generations of human life, moving across the landscape, over eons, and still moving, still walking, still alive, still holding on. Also, I had in mind generations of life passed on genetically—and generations in terms of creativity, generating ideas and theories and hypotheses and art. We speak of electricity being generated. So, a form of energy—generations.

*GJ:* Your poems in earlier collections have often been about recognizing the divine, the sacred, the holy in unexpected places—about a holiness that only comes into existence as the poem witnesses it. I couldn't help thinking as I read *Generations* that there are other things you witness—such as 9/11—and your magnified sense of holiness and divinity, and simple human progress and dignity, evaporates.

*PR:* I wrote the poem "Grief," in *Generations*, for 9/11, though I do not address the event specifically. That poem is fairly dark at the beginning, but there's a turning. I don't think there's a particularly deep or profound thought in the poem. It's two sonnets or composed of two fourteen-line stanzas.

*GJ:* Will you read it?

*PR:* I'd be glad to.

### Grief

Even though, like a stone sinking
in a night sea, it knows depth
and the heavy cloak of darkness; even
though, like a thundercloud in wind,

it is torn apart and reassembled over
and over; even though it draws in,
pulls its ragged edges close around
its central heart, like a blossom
of bindweed at dusk; and even though
its form is as vague and sharp as a shadow
of smoke against a winter hillside;
still it maintains a hard, viable seed
of calm at its core, possesses
the seeking tendency of tendrils

and roots, recalls its lasting kinship
with the past and future wounds
of the living, holds to the heritage
of that certainty, gives itself finally
over to all those powers that rise
by themselves—water oak and willow
saplings, leafy stems of field
thistles, sunflowered and weed-thick
fallows, gatherings of dragonflies,
flockings of warblers, fog in sunlight,
pond turtle and pole star surfacing,
coyote cry of proclamation up
to the moon, and the dominion
of birth, and the kingdom of promise.

*GJ:* It seems that in this poem, as elsewhere in the last section of *Generations*, you're going into some fairly dark places.

*PR:* But "Grief" ends on a positive note. No one is alone in
experiencing grief. To me, that's something one can hold
on to. Everyone living in the past has experienced it—and

it will continue into the future. We hold grief in common with every human being of the past and their power to sustain themselves despite grief.

*GJ:* The poem has that break in the middle—a silence in the middle that seems significant.

*PR:* It is, because that's where the turn happens definitively.

*GJ:* The turn happens right there, but it doesn't feel like a turn initially. You say "the seeking tendency of tendrils" at the end of the first stanza, then you have "and roots . . ." The reader's eye just crosses right over that space. I think in "lasting kinship" we do hear that upward turn. So you wanted that silence in there to accentuate the turn?

*PR:* Yes. "Roots" is an important word, because the action is still "seeking" in the last line of the first stanza, but "roots" suggests being grounded, a more secure and permanent holding.

*GJ:* Yes, I think of a progression, a strengthening of the tendrils, the same holding on.

*PR:* Whether roots or tendrils, there's a measure of certainty. It is certain that grief has a heritage with everyone in the past, and with the future. "Grief" was the only 9/11 poem I wrote, in the sense of writing with that event somewhat in mind. I don't think it's the purview of poetry to address a catastrophic event quickly and directly. Poetry about topical events serves better if it doesn't address the event specifically but rather addresses what rises out of it tangentially.

*GJ:* This poem and "The Ease of Murder" are enormously humane poems. I would say that's true of "God and His People" earlier, too. You're dealing with those things that get in the way of people having a faith. So the title of this last section of the book, "The Following Story," follows . . . what? An arrival at a certain kind of self-consciousness? Or doubt?

*PR:* Perhaps. I suppose all poetry has at its core a further-ance of self-consciousness. Again, "Grief" was written after 9/11, which was a shocking event to me. People who seek death, who proclaim that they are dedicated to seeking death and killing others to maintain that dedication?

*GJ:* I think that in trying to write about the event directly, the poet often ends up mythologizing it—pushing it away instead of bringing it closer, seeing it through all these lenses. I don't know if those lenses are innate in us, but we always do it. We lionize the dead. We're imposing a dis-tance that's supposed to be honorific, but there's something untrue about it.

You told a student at Mercer University when you held the Ferroll Sams Chair there in 2002—he wanted to write about his mother who had died, but he didn't know how— "Just write. And whatever you write in some way will be about her death." I thought that that was a wise answer. Write at a point of deflection from it. Maybe that is true for national as well as personal trauma.

*PR:* Yes, I think so. And poetry has to do something different from prose, in my opinion. After 9/11, everybody was writing prose about that event, the horrific aspect of it, what it meant, how it happened, how to reconcile ourselves to it. So what's poetry going to do that's different, that adds a dimension to the event that prose can't? If you're going to write poetry, you have to think, "What is it that poetry must do that a wonderful essay or a wonderful short story cannot do?" The answer to that question will be different for different poets.

Stanley Plumly's poem "Lapsed Meadow" is a beautiful description of an old, old apple tree in the middle of a field. When you get to the dedication at the bottom, you find that it's for James Wright—written just after Wright died. Plumly never says anything about the death of anybody in that whole poem, and he didn't put the dedication at the top. That, to me, is the way you address a traumatic event in a poem. You say something beautiful about something else that then reflects on the event subtly but stunningly, in the way poetry works.

*GJ:* I think there's a connection of silence there. One of the powers of poetry over prose is the silence that surrounds the former. There's a great deal that's not said, a great deal that you resist. The poem doesn't say the easy thing or try to fill the space between the margins. There's a correspondence between that general silence in poetry and the way the Plumly poem is silent about its chief subject, giving you the apple tree instead—which speaks volumes.

*PR:* The essence of an event and our response to it can't be bound up, captured in language. The words articulated too directly lose all touch with the essence.

*GJ:* I'm curious about "Breaking Old Forms" in *Generations*. Was it written before or after 9/11?

*PR:* Before. It was an effort again to see things in a new way, not to be looking at things in the old ways.

*GJ:* I love the last stanza of this poem. [*reads*]

> If the old form of death could be fully
> understood—a form like naked claws
> latching together mid-breath, a structure
> of falling like furled ice closing
> around the blood of a red blossom—
> then someone might break death apart too
> with a thousand lines aimed perfectly
> at the weld of its network. Or someone
> might simply shatter its structure
> by lifting it carefully with one hand,
> moving it, as if by love, right into the body
> with the other, its decrepit habits
> taken in, encompassed anew, surprised
> by this endearment, coaxed to yield
> to such a gentle form of union.

*PR:* We don't understand what death is. We're locked into a perception of it partly because of the language with which we approach it. One way of breaking out of our perception of it might be through metaphor. I laid out various events in the body of the poem and came back to them in the closing, using them as metaphors for perceiving death in that last stanza. Trying something wholly different for me. "Lifting it carefully with one hand / moving it, as if by love, right into the body / with the other," meeting it with gentleness instead of resisting it when it comes, accepting and embracing it. I'm not referring to suicide, of course. I'm not referring to seeking death but how to perceive it differently and accept it when it comes.

*GJ:* "Encompassed anew"—you taking death in, instead of it taking you in, instead of the old familiar fear of death as the maw.

*PR:* Not a passive acceptance, but something like a welcoming. Suppose you met death, when it came, with endearment and gentleness? Maybe it becomes something else then, something different, I don't know. I was just trying to move beyond a way of thinking that is locked in by language. "Study from Right Angles" was also an attempt to examine death and the transition it brings in a new way for me. The initial investigation in these two poems is, "What is death?" They attempt to look at death anew. These two poems I'm fairly comfortable with.

*GJ:* How about "Who Might Have Said," the last poem of this collection and among my favorites. The fact that it's a final poem imparts a new meaning to the title of the book: the "you" in the poem *generates* this person who walks up out of the river, the savior—who, in turn, reminds me that the title poem, "Generations," opens the book with an upright, ancestral striding:

> They have been walking from the beginning
> through the foggy sponges of lowland
> forests, under umbrella leaves, in the shattered
> rain of ocean beaches, through the tinder
> of ash pits, the thickets of cities. . . .

In all five stanzas of "Generations," the walking continues through an ice age and a meteor shower, through what seems to be an early war, through a total eclipse of the sun, "words let there be light / more than once." The walking seems to imply persistence, evolution, and collective human identity and heritage, though the poem isn't explicit about who the they might be.

Then, "Who Might Have Said" closes the collection beautifully and strongly, opening with an imperative: "Come up out of the river." Throughout this poem an individual is walking, and the walk up out of the river seems post-baptismal.

*PR:* Yes, I mean it to refer to a new birth.

*GJ:* It is rejuvenating, the way the poem calls the reader out of the river. The act of walking seems simple:

> Walk out
> the way fog walks, without significance
> enfolding everything, claiming nothing,
> like the gold of a green brier thicket
> in the dawn claims nothing from the soul.

But I sense an ethical presence here, too—the walker doesn't make claims. "Enfolding everything" eschews the claims to certitude made by religious fundamentalism, made by extremism, authoritarian government, and any group or collective that corners any market. Claiming nothing seems enormously important in the poem. Coming out of the river and "enfolding everything, claiming nothing."

*PR:* Absolutely. Isn't this the way to come anew, isn't this the way to proceed? This is an important poem to me. I've read it to audiences a couple of times, and it doesn't get much reaction. I feel it's very musical. I feel the music of it, and the sound is of urging, encouragement. "Come . . ." Come this way.

*GJ:* I'm surprised. This one feels entirely accessible to me, especially given the last stanza: "Come. Now. You are the one / who understands the way."

*PR:* I don't know why. Maybe it's unsettling in its religious implications. I meant to take my presence out of it by the title. It isn't my voice saying this. It's a poem of hope and confidence in our abilities to . . . I don't know . . . by becoming fully ourselves being enabled to move beyond ourselves. It was significant to me to say this. That next to last stanza was not easy. I thought and thought about that.

*GJ:* The sixth and seventh (which is next to last) stanzas are remarkable:

> Come like the river comes, voluptuous
> with sky, broken and mended again
> by the breaking. Walk out the way the plum
> walks from its blossom, ravaging
> with transfiguration, killing in the way
> a seed always kills.

> Sentient as script, come out of the river
> like *river*. Come the way the savior as *water*
> keeps rising out of the water, keeps walking
> closer and closer as *sea* to the sea.

That's such a reverse of the way we usually think about seed. The seed is fed by death.

*PR:* It loses itself in the process of becoming transfigured. During transfiguration, in which the seed participates, it ceases to be a seed. When something ceases, it's not always a destructive act. It depends on how it happens and what takes its place.

*GJ:* What was difficult about writing that next to last stanza?

*PR:* It was the last sentence. I can't remember the details, but I kept thinking, what was this savior? *River* and *water* and *sea* as words—the Gospel of John starts with the word, and the word was God. So it's important that these words be italicized. The poem is about language but it's also about the savior as the word. He keeps coming, he's eternal, and he keeps walking closer and closer, as *sea* to the sea. Conception becoming reality. What happens when the two become one? Of course, I can't explain it entirely, in the way that music can't be explained.

*GJ:* The sections of *Generations* are ordered as a series of stories—"The First Story," "The Second Story," until, following "The Fifth Story," the book culminates with "The Following Story." I was interested in the distinction between the ordinal numbers and the word "following."

*PR:* I titled that last section "The Following Story" because I thought it suggested not an ending but a continuation. To have titled it "The Sixth Story" would have implied just another story, or a conclusion. *Generations* is in many ways about motion, all kinds of motion; the first section is about physical motion, about continuation, about the ongoing, about generating, and I meant the last section to suggest that continuation.

GJ: In many of your poems, there's an emphasis on the organs and the vehicles of perception. In "In Order to Perceive," from your first book, for instance, perception only works if there is a suggestion that leads to enormous visions—even some visions, by the end of the poem, that the reader is starting to doubt a little bit because they become so grand. I want you to talk about your concerns about the organs of perception, and the way I think we often take those organs for granted. We don't recognize that to some degree they see what they're taught to see.

PR [*flipping though* Generations *until she stops on pages 47 and 48*]: These two poems, "The Questing" and "Seeing What Is Seen," are similar to "In Order to Perceive," which is an earlier poem and more difficult for me to remember writing. "The Questing" and "Seeing What Is Seen" actually were written about the same time; one followed the other.

GJ: And they follow each other in *Generations*.

PR: I had this idea that we see by being seen, that we perceive and define ourselves partly by being witnessed by our surroundings. I didn't say that in this poem specifically, but there is a perception you gain by being around other creatures: when a cat looks at you and you see the cat looking at you, all of a sudden you are defined by the cat. You see yourself as the cat might see you. When a creature looks you directly in the eye, and you're looking at it, something happens. You know something about yourself that you didn't know before. You're being perceived in a different way by a different sort of perception.

*GJ:* That's another way you're seeing yourself from out-side yourself. "Hearing the Unexpected" in *Song of the World Becoming* (2001) says, "In time, the ear may be capable / of hearing its own function." There's a self-consciousness that you come around to. It seems to me there's always another consciousness to arrive at in the poems. You treat the ear almost as if it has a selfhood entirely apart from the rest of the body. And that's true in *Generations*, too. You have a lot of poems about ears and hearing, and a lot of poems about seeing, being seen, the faculty of sight. But in "Hearing the Unexpected," I think you arrive at this ultimate moment of self-consciousness where the ear can be brought to know its own meaning. And I guess that's the ultimate upshot of self-consciousness. Is it?

*PR:* Self-consciousness in general, meaning and function? Yes, I suppose that's true. In regard to this particular poem and the investigation of the ear in many of its manifesta-tions, that's just where the poem seemed to be going. And it seemed like an interesting trail being created. There's a great deal to say about how we tend to see, and hear, only what has been pointed out to us, as in the poem "In Order to Perceive." We are given words for those things that are pointed out to us. What about everything else? What are we missing? That's one reason why I like poetry, because it allows me to surmise, to question what may be beyond what we presently see and hear simply because it's never been noticed. It's never been named.

*GJ:* Turning back to *Generations*, I want to ask you about "On the Eve of the Hearing," which seems to do all in one poem of four or five movements what it took you several poems to do earlier in your career. The poem ends with the same human foreground that's so distinctive throughout the collection. The one-word sentence "Listen" at the end reflects what I think might be the key imperative in all your poems: stop asserting, and listen to what possible answers are there. *All* the possible answers, not just the ones already offered up by the culture or by the purveyors of culture.

*PR:* Yes, exactly.

*GJ:* The poem begins, as your work often does, with an experience of the body, the experience of the ear:

> The ear being boneless and almost always
> exposed, except in icy, windy weather,
> possesses a rather charming vulnerability,
> an innocent faith in the purpose of its presence.
> Never changing its strange expression,
> it waits patiently, a pure *waiting* in the flesh
> to apprehend all sounds coming its way,
> the creaks and whines, the bangs and chirps
> of the universe roiling and bubbling.

These are sounds it has learned to hear as well as sounds it has yet to learn to catch. Then the poem moves into a narrative experience: ". . . I once knew a woman / whose cat sucked the lobe of her ear," and "Lovers often seek the earlobe this way, too." That's very rich, even erotic in the description of the lovers. You have "the vestige of a remote ancestor" in there, so there's the human pre-history, which is also suggested in the image of the warrior who made a necklace of the ears of his victims. If that's pre-history, then you have post-history in the Gethsemane story of Peter and Malchus, the soldier whose ear Christ heals. And for good measure you have a human ear grown on the back of a lab mouse, and "Some babies have been born with ears closed tight . . ." It seems to me that in this one poem there is a condensation of all the important things you've been trying to do. Were you thinking that as you wrote it?

*PR:* Not specifically, but I did intend each section to examine the ear in a different way. But I guess it would be inevitable that if I were to pick a subject, I would go through various ways of considering it. I think the third section is unique to *Generations* in its appreciation of our ancestry, our ancestry from the beginning, both what we've inherited physically and what we've inherited culturally.

*GJ:* I like this passage from "On the Eve of the Hearing": ". . . Touch / that old, old vanished kin, the dim / and perished who bore, the living ghost / you own, but may never remember."

*PR:* We don't know everything that we have inherited from these generations that went before us—which is another meaning of *Generations*. Even though we may know about this fold in the outer ear that has been inherited from primitive ancestors, we don't know everything we possess from them. We don't know everything. But we are linked—no, not just linked, but *bound physically* to our oldest ancestors, to pre-history.

*GJ:* I couldn't help but think about documentaries I've seen in which archaeologists digging in a particular place use DNA evidence to trace ancestry to see if people living there now are actual descendants or genetic inheritors of the fossil remains that date back several thousand years. They've done this in England. And they found people who didn't know they had this long-standing connection to the landscape but actually do. I find that just remarkable.

*PR:* I know. It's just another connection that binds us to all kinds of details in the physical world we live in, connections we haven't been aware of before, like the fact that our bodies are made of the dust of old stars. It seems more and more difficult to put ourselves outside the earth, the world, the universe we live in—we're so intimately connected to it all. I find that vision sustaining, energizing, and comforting.

*GJ:* I also wonder about the end of "On the Eve of Hearing," where "The ear has its own stories, / its own myths. Listen." At the end of the poem we're listening to ears.

*PR [laughing]:* Yes.

*GJ:* We're waiting for the ear to tell, we're waiting for the hearing appendage to speak. I don't know what sort of take on reciprocal creation that is, but I kept thinking of—this is just me, this doesn't rise to me from the poem although you mention Gethsemane in the stanza—the story of someone asking Mother Teresa not long before she died how she prayed, and she said, "I just listen." The interviewer asked, "What does God say?" and she said, "He just listens, too."

PR: Oh! Yes, I like that.

GJ: I have the same kind of moment at the end of your poem, as I'm listening to what listening itself is.

PR: Yes.

GJ: There's a concentricity of silence here that I think is very appealing and unusual.

When we talked another time, you mentioned *Splitting and Binding* as your favorite of your books. Is that still true?

PR: Well, not my favorite, but one of the best organized and most coherent, I believe, in its approach and stance.

GJ: I remember a critic saying you had fully realized in that collection the possibilities of the poem as supposition.

PR: That may be true, too. I just like it because there aren't any poems in it that I regret. *Splitting and Binding* is a good length. It's fairly short—three poems each in nine sections, so twenty-seven poems.

GJ: You just implied that there are some poems in other books that you regret. What are some of those?

PR: Well, I don't believe I'll give you any specific titles; I'll just say a few contain some kind of flaw or other, in my opinion. I often tell my students that if they haven't risked anything in the poem, if they haven't walked on a very narrow edge where there's always the possibility of falling off at any moment and appearing foolish, then the poem will probably not be worth much. But you can't let the fear of falling and appearing foolish stop you from taking significant risks in the poem. Someone who epitomizes, for me, taking risks in his poems is Theodore Roethke. Not all of his poems are a success, but he's almost always taking risks, searching, questing—and not just risks at being clever with craft or form, but risks in reaching for something vague but significant. Whether he gets there or he fails and sounds foolish, he has made a grand effort at trying to confront something important. I admire him for the risks that he's taken with language, the things that he has brought together in his language. I think of him when I'm fearful that I may make a fool of myself.

*GJ:* I think it was Roethke who said if you're not risking sentimentality, you're not close to your interior life—or maybe it was Richard Hugo in *The Triggering Town.*

*PR:* Sounds more like Hugo. But a poet has to know when the risks she chooses to make are the right risks, risks that open the theme or subject to rich possibilities.

*GJ:* I see a lot of sympathy in your poems for some awful things humans used to do. "The Dead Never Fight Against Anything"—I love that poem. I'm horrified by it, but I love it because of what it articulates about the ancestors and because of the way you end it: "pitiless, pitiless betrayal." That's a sign and a weapon for the living against the dead.

It's an affirmation of one part of grief that I don't think we like to acknowledge—the anger that comes with it.

PR: I struggled with some of the poems and their themes in *Generations*, or rather the poems themselves are about struggling.

GJ: Were there poems in this book that *did* come easily? I wonder about "The Match."

PR: Easily in terms of my being comfortable, satisfied with it when I thought I was through? "The Match" in that sense was easy. It didn't come quickly, but I liked the direction the poem was taking, the focus on the struggle between two strong forces, neither identified, and how they determine each other. "Servant, Birthright" I know was written after 9/11. "The Body and the Soul" was written in 2000. "Bearings on a Winter Evening"—that's a dark poem—was written after 9/11.

GJ: The cave diving is a living burial in that poem. It's bleak, dark, and harrowing, that kind of travel.

PR: Yes—travel, motion again. It's also a poem examining imagination. Which one of the scenes described in the poem is in the speaker's imagination? Is the speaker underground imagining she's sitting and watching out a window, or is she watching out a window imagining she's underground? But whichever scene is the reality, it's not particularly promising.

GJ: There's an intense cold in that poem.

*PR:* Very cold. Even the speaker, ostensibly inside looking out on a winter scene, is cold. I keep seeing her curled up and wrapped in a blanket. Nothing bright about it.

*GJ:* I think "Servant, Birthright" takes some risks. "God and His People" does too. I understand what you mean about the larger book. But the book occasionally feels to me—and I've read almost all your other work—as if you're coming into another kind of poem. You're moving toward another kind of writing that you're not certain about yet.

*PR:* I agree with that. There's a little uncertainty or tentativeness in some of the poems in this book. I'm questioning much of my previous work . . . well, reassessing it is better, more accurate. What have I omitted that needs to be there? I want to know. What have I not addressed clearly? What can I approach from a different direction? What have I failed to celebrate?

*GJ:* I wonder whether you sense any of your own unconscious operating in "The Match." That's a violent poem. Real combat is going on—a tenacious wrestling match between two aging women who "Were they to cease, to part, / were they to surrender or subdue, neither / would have a name, no spine of hell, / no hard grasp of heaven." I can't help but, in the context of what you've said today, think about that poem as a defining struggle. The poem isn't confessional, but I sense in it a personal struggle for definition.

You've found something that you're not as an artist, as a person, anymore. You're not the nature poet that you've been made into. You're uncertain about your roles in these other pretty important dimensions. The important things for you, you've said, the first things, have been mothering and then writing. And here you're kind of at a loss as to what a grandmother is supposed to be. And you're at a loss as to what writing and culture have really accomplished in a world where 9/11 can happen.

*PR:* Absolutely right. You have really said it better than I could. I have some doubt too about where we are as a species, the strength of our ability to control our destructive instincts, our ability to express our spiritual instincts and draw on them for strength and guidance.

For many months after 9/11, when I gave readings, I didn't feel entirely like the celebratory voice of my earlier poems. And yet those were the poems I knew the audience wanted to hear. That was the basic tone of all my work. I still believed in that voice, the importance of that voice, and yet sometimes I felt dishonest, like an imposter, because I was worried and uncertain about how we would face these new threats and worried that all the endeavors of our culture in the arts and sciences, our ideals of freedom, might be lost. But sometimes, strangely enough, my own poems, along with the response of the audience, would rejuvenate me during a reading. And I realized again something I'd been saying for a long time—that praise is often an expression of sorrow and uncertainty. Praise is an acknowledgment of the ephemeral nature of all that surrounds us and the love we feel for all that is of value, and yet vulnerable, in our lives.

*GJ:* And also that we can declare the really holy things holy. That we can get at what's really holy, and enlarge our definition of the holy and the sacred. And of course that faith was undercut by 9/11, which turned everything upside down.

*PR:* Osama bin Laden said, "We love death. The U.S. loves life. That is the big difference between us." That kind of thinking is what can happen when you latch onto any fundamentalist belief too rigidly and shut out all questioning of yourself and your beliefs, when you quit searching, when you believe you know absolute truth. It's crucial for us to remember, every one of us, that a great deal of the time we are all foolish, silly creatures. Yet once in a while one or another of us manages to rise up and touch something gloriously clear, pure, wondrous, and full of life and being, and we need to do everything we can to make those moments possible. That means first maintaining freedom of expression, maintaining the widest freedom possible for the imagination.

*GJ:* I think what you just said elucidates some of the difficulties in *Generations*. I can't help but think in a new way about the emphasis of the book on generations—generations of people, generating culture, generating art. There's a sense of progression in the title poem itself: "walking . . . walking" toward something. I can't help but think of that in both evolutionary and ethical terms. But here is this moment where we seem to have just grown tails all over again.

*PR:* . . . as if no progress has been made since our first early ancestor picked up a stone and killed someone with it.

Perhaps it was naïve ever to have considered that as a species we had made progress in moderating our destructive impulses. Or, more likely, we make progress and then regress.

*GJ:* So where do you go, in your poems, if your whole poetry has been predicated on a sense of growing light, on a sense of human progression—moral, ethical, and otherwise—when there's suddenly that step back?

*PR:* I believe those of us who are writing poetry must keep writing as honestly, as creatively, as imaginatively as possible, just as poets who lived before us kept writing, many of them through very dire times. And now we have their work. Poems addressing the ramifications of 9/11 were already here, those poems written in other times, by other poets facing other crises.

I remember reading an Emily Dickinson poem to an audience on the day of the Oklahoma City bombing, and it addressed the feelings surrounding that event perfectly—Dickinson having written that poem with no knowledge of the Oklahoma City bombing except its deepest significance. She understood what poetry is.

As I've said, poetry does not, and I might say should not, address directly very specific geopolitical events. That approach limits the range of the poem, because it comes from a mind-set with a fixed agenda. Where the poem is going is predictable, both to writer and to reader. Poetry should address the value of human life. As Faulkner said on receiving the Nobel Prize, "It is [the poet's] privilege to help man endure by lifting his heart, by reminding him of the courage and honor and hope and pride and compassion and pity and sacrifice which have been the glory of his past."

Think again of this earth, this tiny earth, a tiny, tiny pearl floating in this whole mass of exploding gases and nebulae, of stars being born and dying. Our precious earth traveling with a kind of strange and touching faith beside an ordinary star, one of billions, in just an ordinary galaxy, one of billions.

We have to see ourselves, our noble actions and our insane violence, from this perspective. What does that vision mean to our morality, our spiritual needs? How does it affect what we value? We all know the vision of that perspective is there; we've seen those pictures of the earth. And yet it's as if we were afraid to look at them, afraid to comprehend the implications of those images, afraid to take them into our hearts and our lives and incorporate them into our definition of who we might be in this place where we find ourselves.

I believe there is a significant purpose to our existence, our yearnings, our affinity for beauty and light, and to our unique awareness of ourselves, although we aren't yet able to express fully that purpose. "When there's suddenly that step back . . ." where does poetry go? What do poets do? We continue to write as diligently and courageously as possible, we continue to seek and to question, we continue to celebrate the universe. We must accept this life with the same generosity as the generosity exhibited through its gift to us.

(2005)

# Acknowledgments and Credits

*Georgia Review*, "Breaking Old Forms: A Conversation with Gordon Johnston," used by permission of Gordon Johnston.

*Image*, "Born, Again and Again"; "Poems That Possess Me Like New Music in the Blood: An Interview with Brian Doyle," used by permission of Brian Doyle.

*In Brief*, edited by Judith Kitchen and Mary Paumier Johes (W. W. Norton), "Fury and Grace"

*Iowa Review*, "An Interview with Richard McCann," copyright © 1987 by Richard McCann. Originally appeared in the *Iowa Review* 17, no. 2 (Spring–Summer 1987). Reprinted by permission of Brandt & Hochman Literary Agents, Inc.

Robinson Jeffers, "Epic Stars" from *The Collected Poetry of Robinson Jeffers*, Volume 3, edited by Timothy Hunt. Copyright 1954, © 1963 by Donnan and Garth Jeffers. All rights reserved. Used with the permission of Stanford University Press, www.sup.org.

Richard Katrovas, "Star Boys" from *Green Dragons* (Wesleyan University Press, 1983). Copyright © by Richard Katrovas. Used by permission of the author.

*Manoa*, "Places within Place"

*MidAmerican Review*, "The Great Plains"

Milkweed Editions, "This Nature," "Places within Place," and "Surprised by the Sacred," from *The Dream of the Marsh Wren: Writing as Reciprocal Creation* (Minneapolis: Milkweed Editions, 1999). Copyright © 1999 by Pattiann Rogers. Reprinted by permission of Milkweed Editions (www.milkweed.org).

*Northern Lights*, "Thoreau and Mothers"

*Orion*, "Cradle," "Death and the Garden"

*Orion Society Notebook*, "What among Heavens and Suns"

*Portland*, "Rain," "For Me Mothers and the Mothers of Mothers . . . ," "This Nature," "I Hear and Behold God in Every Object, Yet Understand God Not in the Least"

Claudius Ptolemaeus, excerpt from "Star Gazing," translated by Dudley Fitts, from *Poems from the Greek Anthology*. Copyright © 1956 by New Directions Publishing Corp. Reprinted by permission of New Directions Publishing Corp.

Rainer Maria Rilke, "Evening" from *The Selected Poetry of Rainer Maria Rilke*, edited and translated by Stephen Mitchell. Copyright © 1982 by Stephen Mitchell. Used by permission of Random House, Inc.

*Spiritus*, "Small and Insignificant, Mighty and Glorious," copyright © 2002 by the Johns Hopkins University Press. This article first appeared in *Spiritus: A Journal of Christian Spirituality* 2, no. 2 (Fall 2002), 143–46.

*U.S. Catholic*, "Surprised by the Sacred," "A Terrible Need," "A Covenant with Divinity"

*Writing It Down for James* (Beacon Press), "Twentieth-Century Cosmology and the Soul's Habitation"

"For Me Mothers and the Mothers of Mothers . . ." was awarded a bronze medal for feature writing from the Council for the Advancement and Support of Education (International Trade Association for University Work).

"I Hear and Behold God in Every Object, Yet Understand God Not in the Least" appears in *Best Spiritual Writing 2010*, edited by Philip Zaleski (Penguin).

"Born, Again and Again" appears in *Bearing the Mystery: Twenty Years of Image*, edited by Gregory Wolfe (Wm. B. Eerdmans, 2009).

My thanks to Barbara Ras for her astute reading of this manuscript, her insightful editorial suggestions, and her expert guidance of these pieces through the process toward the finished book. Special thanks to my dear friend Brian Doyle who has given encouragement and support during the writing of these essays and whose own essays have provided excellent examples for me. I am extremely grateful to the Lannan Foundation for support and encouragement during the many years when these essays were being written.

PATTIANN ROGERS has published eleven books of poetry; a book-length essay collection, *The Dream of the Marsh Wren;* and *A Covenant of Seasons*, poems and monotypes, in collaboration with the artist Joellyn Duesberry. Her most recent books are *Wayfare* (Penguin, 2008) and *Firekeeper: Selected Poems* (Milkweed Editions, 2005, revised and expanded edition). Rogers is the recipient of two NEA grants, a Guggenheim Fellowship, and a 2005 Literary Award in Poetry from the Lannan Foundation. Among other awards, her poems have won three prizes from *Poetry*, the Roethke Prize from *Poetry Northwest*, two Strousse Awards from *Prairie Schooner*, and five Pushcart Prizes. Her poems have appeared in *The Best American Poetry* (1996, 2010) and in *The Best Spiritual Writing* (1999, 2000, 2001, 2002). An essay appears in the 2010 edition of *The Best Spiritual Writing*. In 2000 Rogers was a resident at the Rockefeller Foundation's Bellagio Study and Conference Center in Bellagio, Italy. Her papers are archived in the Sowell Family Collection of Literature, Community, and the Natural World at Texas Tech University. Rogers has been a visiting writer at numerous universities and colleges and was an associate professor at the University of Arkansas from 1993 to 1997. She is the mother of two sons and has three grandsons. She lives with her husband, a retired geophysicist, in Colorado.